Prayers
for
People Under Pressure

Prayers
for
People Under Pressure

BY

JONATHAN AITKEN

continuum
LONDON • NEW YORK

Continuum
The Tower Building, 11 York Road, London SE1 7NX
15 East 26th Street, New York, NY 10010

www.continuumbooks.com

First published 2005

British Library Cataloguing-in-Publication Data
A catalogue record for this book is available from the British Library.

ISBN 0-8264-7639-2

Typeset in Postscript Sabon by Tony Lansbury, Tonbridge, Kent.
Printed and bound by Creative Print and Design Group, Wales.

To Elizabeth,

my nearest, dearest and closest prayer partner

CONTENTS

PART I: JOURNEY INTO PRAYER   1

PART II: PRAYERS OF ADORATION   23

King David's Prayer of Adoration   24
Psalm 95   26
Short Prayers of Adoration   28
A Prayer in Adoration of the Creator of the Universe   32
Two Hymns of Adoration   34
Prayers for Starting the Day   36–39
Set Our Hearts on Fire   40

PART III: PRAYERS OF CONFESSION   43

A Prayer for God's Help as we Examine our Consciences   44
A General Confession at Morning Prayer   46
A Prayer for Humility in Confession   48
King David's Prayer of Penitence   50
A Confession of Envy   52
Forgive our Foolish Ways   54
An Armenian Prayer for God's Mercy   56
The Denial and Repentance of Peter   58
A General Confession Before Taking Communion   60
Forgive Us for Spoiling Life at Home   62
No Excuses   64
Two Prayers for the Avoidance of Sin, by Søren Kierkegaard   66
A Prayer for Our Pain to Become Our Healing   68
The Paradox of Repentance   70
Two Prayers for Forgiveness, by John Donne   72–75
The Jesus Prayer   76
The Prayer Of Commitment   78

PART IV: PRAYERS OF THANKSGIVING   81

A Call To Give Thanks   82
St Paul's Prayer of Thanksgiving for God's Grace   84
Two Prayers for a Grateful Heart   86

In Thanksgiving for Answered Prayer   88
General Thanksgiving   90

PART V: PRAYERS FOR OUR RELATIONSHIP WITH GOD   93

Two Prayers of St Clement   94
A Prayer for the Cleansing of Our Hearts   96
A Prayer for the Royalty of Inward Happiness   98
A Prayer of Human Uncertainty and Godly Trust   100
A Prayer to Grow in Faith   102
Martin Luther's Prayer on Emptiness and Weakness of Faith   104
A Prayer to Stay Connected With God   106
A Prayer for Self Control   108
Shut Out Everything Except God   110
To Care Only for God's Approval   112
A Prayer for Perseverance   114
Augustine's Prayer for Purity of Heart   116
Three Crucial Questions   118
A Prayer for God's Mercy, Peace and Grace   120

PART VI: HOW NOT TO PRAY   123

1. How Not to Pray   124

PART VII: SUPPLICATION   129

 1. A Prayer for a Sense of Humour   130
 2. A 17th-Century Nun's Prayer   132
 3. A Prayer for Listening   134
 4. The Prayer of Jabez   136
 5. A Prayer to Avoid Bad Temper   138
 6. Two Prayers about Fear   140–142
 7. Two Prayers Before Taking Exams   144–147
 8. A Prayer About Fear of Flying   148
 9. Prayer for Going through Divorce   150
10. A Prayer for Dealing with Enemies   152
11. A Parent's Prayer for a Teenager Suffering from
        an Eating Disorder   154
12. A Prayer for Sleep   156
13. A Prayer for Life and Work   158
14. Prayers for Work   160–163
15. A Prayer for the Sighing of the Prisoner   164
16. Charles Colson's Prayer for those in Prison   166
17. A Prayer for Prisoners of Conscience   168

18. A Prayer for All Prisoners   170
19. A Prayer for Victims of Crime   172
20. Help me to Pray ... Restore me to Liberty   174
21. The Prayer for Parliament   176
22. A Prayer for The United States Senate   178
23. In Times of Pain   180
24. A Prayer for those who Wake or Watch or Weep Tonight   182
25. Finding God When Close to Death   184
26. When the Fever of Life is Over   186
27. A Prayer in Times of Sudden Bereavement   188
28. Five Prayers for those that Mourn   190–193
29. John Donne's Vision of Heaven   194

Acknowledgements   197

PART I

Journey Into Prayer

'I know you're having a terrible time. Can I come in and pray with you?' said the man standing on my doorstep. It was the summer of 1997 and I was under tremendous pressure from media stakeouts and scrutiny. So I hesitated, fearing that this might be yet another ingenious ploy by a reporter to get inside the house. After some suspicious peering at the entryphone screen I recognised the man on the doorstep. He was a distant acquaintance, Mervyn Thomas. I remembered that he had recently written me a sympathetic letter about the disastrous collapse of my libel action against *The Guardian*. I did not have many sympathisers in those dark days. So, on impulse, I let him in.

In the conversation that followed Mervyn Thomas made it clear that what he had really meant on the doorstep was that he wanted to pray *out loud* with me. Belonging as I then did to the church reticent wing of Anglicanism I would rather have gone to the dentist without an anaesthetic. However, the combination of my terrible times and my guest's sympathy weakened my resistance. So Mervyn did pray aloud and I half-heartedly joined in the 'Amen'. It was my first experience of one-on-one extempore oral prayer.

'Would you like me to come again?' asked Mervyn Thomas.

'Well ... er ... yes ... no ... I don't think this kind of thing is really my scene ... I mean, I wouldn't like to do it too often,' I muttered.

'But I think you do need regular prayer support,' was the gentle response.

Regular prayer support. It was the second time the phrase had crossed my horizon in the past few days. Its first appearance came in a letter from a political acquaintance offering to convene a group of 'friends from Parliamentary and public life' who would meet once a week to give me 'regular prayer support'. The writer of this letter was Michael Alison. Good, solid, dependable old Michael. Eton, Cambridge, the Brigade of Guards, Tory MP, junior Health Minister, Willie Whitelaw's No. 2 as Minister of State for Northern Ireland,

Margaret Thatcher's Parliamentary Private Secretary, Privy Councillor, Church Commissioner and a quintessentially loyal senior back-bencher. I was on friendly terms with him but not close. A few months earlier I had asked him if a press story saying that he had refused a knighthood was true. 'Well, yes, I didn't really feel worthy of it', was his reply, which I thought bordered on the eccentric considering how many far less worthy parliamentary colleagues collect their 'Ks' with the rations.

I knew Michael was a practising Christian because he was a regular attender at the Communion service for MPs held monthly in St Margaret's, Westminster, followed afterwards by breakfast in Speaker's House. However, there were no clues from his self-effacing conversation at these events to suggest that Michael could be into 'praying out loud' or any other deviations from traditional religion, such as forming groups to provide fallen sinners with 'regular prayer support'. It sounded a step too far from the C. of E. that I knew. So I stayed cool and reticent about the idea.

In their different ways, Mervyn Thomas and Michael Alison stayed warm and persistent. They had an unexpected American ally in Charles Colson, with whom I was exchanging deeply personal letters that summer. Notorious for being Richard Nixon's 'hatchet man', who had served a jail sentence for Watergate-related offences, Colson had been a valuable source of new material for my 1993 biography of the 37th President of the United States. In my historical interviews with Colson about the goings-on in the Nixon White House he had barely mentioned his post-Watergate conversion to a life of Christian faith and ministry. Even so, we struck up a good rapport and he reviewed my book generously in the American press. However, we were no longer in touch with each other until, by chance, Colson was staying in a London hotel on 21st June 1997, the day when I became front-page news as public enemy number one after being caught out telling a lie on oath in the *Guardian* libel case.

Colson immediately wrote me a letter urging me to take the Christian path of repentance. Filled with remorse for my wrong-doing, I was receptive to his suggestion. However, I had no real understanding of the concept of repentance. I did not know the deeper meaning of the Greek word for it, *metanoia*, which translates as 'a change of heart and mind'. I thought repentance consisted of saying sorry, preferably as quietly and as privately as possible, and then getting back to business as usual.

As my correspondence with Colson developed, he seemed to be suggesting a far less convenient approach to repentance. He recommended that I should 'get a group of praying friends' around me to whom I should 'become accountable'. He mentioned his own experiences described in full in his 1976 autobiography, *Born Again*, of belonging to a group which consisted of a Senator, two Congressmen and a Washington DC pastor. This quartet breakfasted together once a week, 'shared everything as brothers' and 'had fellowship' – whatever that was. This formula of Born Againers sharing coffee, croissants, sins and Bible reading had no appeal for me. My religion was private and was going to stay that way.

For some weeks there was a tug-of-war in my spiritual life between privacy and fellowship. It was resolved not by Evangelical Protestants but by Roman Catholics. Long before I was in any kind of trouble I had developed a friendship with Father Gerard Hughes SJ, the author of *God of Surprises*. We had met when my political star was in the ascendant and the skies of my ambition seemed cloudless. At that time I was so keen on worldly success that I was not particularly receptive to what he called 'spiritual direction'. However, there must have been the seeds of a latent spiritual hunger buried somewhere deep within me. For against my natural instincts and in defiance of the pressures of a Cabinet Minister's diary, Father Hughes somehow persuaded me to participate in the first ever parliamentary retreat in Lent 1994, a commitment which meant setting aside several hours a week for the various activities this involved.

During the retreat we talked a lot about prayer, which Father Hughes defined as 'daring to make the inner journey'. Later he added that there were times in the journey when one needed companions and there were times when one needed to pray alone. On that basis there was no need for any tug-of-war between what my self-defence mechanism called 'private religion' and what Messrs Colson, Alison and Thomas variously called 'fellowship', 'prayer partnership' or 'prayer support group' religion. Even so I was still equivocal about getting involved with such novel (for me) activities, until one night I was reading a retreat on prayer by Evelyn Underhill who quoted some advice from a 16th-century Catholic mystic, St Teresa of Avila. The advice was, 'when you start to pray, get yourself some company'. This sentence hit me like a killer punch, knocking out my already fading resistance to Michael Alison's proposal of 'a prayer support group' to help me through my troubles.

The group that duly convened for breakfast, Bible reading and prayer every Thursday morning consisted of what appeared to be a gathering of reserved, cautious and determinedly non-intrusive Englishmen. In alphabetical order we were: Jonathan Aitken, Michael Alison, Tom Benyon (all ex-MPs); Alastair Burt, a sitting MP[1]; Anthony Cordle, the son of a former MP; Michael Hastings, a senior BBC executive; James Pringle, a retired businessman; and, later on, Mervyn Thomas. How Michael Alison got this lot together remains something of a mystery. I myself knew none of them well and three of them not at all. The only common denominator was that they were all willing to turn up once a week to pray for someone in trouble.

Although my troubles were getting steadily worse, unfolding into the nightmare scenario of defeat, disgrace, divorce, bankruptcy and jail, the dynamics of this prayer group soon took on a life that went deeper and wider than the Aitken dramas.

Until I joined this group my idea of praying was to say the Lord's Prayer, occasionally adding one or two 'Lord, help me!' mumbles of an entirely self-centred nature. On a bad day I might possibly open the 1662 Book of Common Prayer and read whichever of its versicles, responses, prayers or collects seemed particularly appropriate to my circumstances. Although some of the BCP's liturgical creations have great power and beauty, such a formal style of prayer can easily become stilted and depersonalised. So I was ready to enlarge my prayer horizons even if the new prayer techniques to which I was being introduced came as quite a surprise.

The most regular of these techniques was to go round the table at our Thursday breakfasts, asking: 'What are your prayer needs?' Once we had broken through the barriers of British reserve with each other, this question brought to the surface all manner of replies in areas such as family worries, job or money pressures, personal relationship problems and so on. 'What are your prayer needs?' may sound a mundane question, but the oral prayers that flowed from it were sometimes remarkable, as were the answers to those prayers.

We were fortunate that our group included some experienced believers with great gifts of prayer. For example James Pringle, who had a voice like a cello and an encyclopaedic knowledge of the Bible, had rare skills in linking our prayer requests to passages of scripture.

---

1. Alastair Burt is now Parliamentary Private Secretary to the Rt Hon Michael Howard MP, Leader of the Opposition.

Mervyn Thomas, an experienced Baptist pastor, brought a fervour to prayer that I had never before experienced. Michael Alison changed from a pillar of the Anglican establishment into a sage of Reform theology (a subject he had studied at Ridley Hall, Cambridge), using his learning to lead our Bible readings with great expertise. The rest of us joined in with far less scriptural knowledge and devotional experience but, even so, the totality of the group's prayerfulness somehow felt powerful.

These Thursday breakfasts made two important impacts on me. The first was that the word 'Brothers', or in its longer form 'Brothers in Christ', took on a real meaning. Although we were very different characters our unity of purpose turned us into a fraternal group of loving prayer partners within a matter of weeks. Jesus' words: 'When two or three are gathered together in my name, there am I in the midst of them,' cast their own mantle over us all, so much so that there were times during our prayers when I felt his presence to be near. This strong feeling of being part of a brotherhood of Christ's followers had its effect on my prayers. I stopped asking for God's holy electrical energy to come down from the skies to solve my problems, to stop me from being prosecuted, going to jail, losing my house and so on. Instead, I prayed for my brothers (whose private troubles sometimes seemed almost as needful as my public torments) and for the requests they had made on behalf of their families, their friends and their situations. This seismic shift away from self-centred prayer towards praying for others was swiftly followed by the second impact of belonging to the group. The more I heard about Jesus Christ from our Bible studies and prayers, the greater became my desire to learn more about him. I felt his powerful attraction, perhaps even his call (though I did not recognise it at the time) and so I prayed to get to know him better.

This new shift towards God-seeking prayer met with an unexpected response from Michael Alison. He told me that he had been a former churchwarden of a leading evangelical church in London: Holy Trinity, Brompton, which ran classes in Christian teaching called Alpha courses. He said I should do one. At that time I had heard neither of the church, nor of the course. But I trusted Michael so, at his instigation, I went to see the Vicar of Holy Trinity, Brompton. He was not the rabid hot-gospeller I had somehow been expecting to meet. He was a reassuringly avuncular figure, the Revd Sandy Millar whom, 40 years earlier, I had thought of as an icon because when I was a small boy at Eton he had been a school prefect or Member of Pop. As the heroes of one's youth can be the heroes of one's life it did not seem as strange as it might otherwise have done for me to be sitting in Sandy's vicarage study receiving his godly wisdom, which seemed to come down to: 'If you're serious about having a relationship with Jesus you should come and do an Alpha course here at HTB.'

When I found out what an Alpha course was, I did everything I could to avoid it. A cover story in *The Spectator* by Christine Odone on Alpha was published a week before the 1997 autumn course began. It was a hatchet job, caricaturing Alpha as an extremist sect for the Hooray Henrys and Henriettas of Chelsea and Kensington who enjoyed swooning in the aisles, confessing their sins in groups and empowering themselves with the Holy Spirit to make more money. I promptly tried to back out of the course I had signed up for, but a surprisingly steely Michael Alison persuaded me to stick to the plan. As I was still wavering on the night the Alpha course began, his persuasion took the form of physically escorting me to Holy Trinity, Brompton, where I felt out of place, uncomfortable and unpleasantly notorious. The only reason I could think of for being there was that I had made a bad call of judgement out of good manners to Michael Alison and Sandy Millar.

I found the Alpha course far more orthodox, interesting and congenial than I had expected. These reactions had much to do with the quality of the talks given by the Alpha chaplain, Nicky Gumbel, and the normality of the people who were in our group, which was led by Bruce Streather, a solicitor and amateur golfing champion who in time was to become one of my closest friends. However, despite the good preaching of Gumbel and the good company of Streather, I do not think I would have lasted for the duration of the ten-week course had it not been for the fifth talk, entitled 'How Do I Pray?' It was given, not by an ordained clergyman, but by a young woman in a mini-skirt called Jo Glenn. It was her message rather than her mini-skirt which captivated me, for by the end of the evening my searchings had taken a new turn towards something my spiritual life had sorely lacked – prayer discipline.

What the *How Do I Pray?* talk of the Alpha course suggested was that prayer can benefit from having a structure. The one recommended was a four-part structure under the headings: Adoration, Confession, Thanksgiving and Supplication. Other ideas included setting a fixed time each day for prayer, keeping a prayer diary and persevering with prayer through all disappointments and setbacks. I cannot explain why Jo Glenn's talk spoke to me, but it did. I tried her recommendations and they started to work. Within days I was settling down to a regular, disciplined prayer life using the ACTS format.

Although I did not understand it at the time, the Alpha course talk on prayer had set me off on a momentous journey. One of my first discoveries was that each one of the initials in the ACTS acronym requires a voyage of exploration of its own. So I began with Adoration, a spiritual subject I had hitherto considered for approximately two seconds a year on Christmas Day when singing the 'O come, let us adore him' line from *O come, all ye faithful*.

But what is adoration? I now think of it as the starter motor of prayer, the energiser of all our requests and communications to God. For how can we hope to receive Our Lord's gifts and mercies if we fail to transmit to him our love, reverence and praise? If one believes this, one starts to search for the right thoughts and language with which to express adoration. Soon my prayer diary was filling up with my own and other people's attempts at responding to this challenge. As a result, a selection of prayers of adoration fills the first 20 pages of the main body of this book.

T. S. Eliot wrote in his poem, *The Love Song of Alfred J. Prufrock*: 'I have measured out my life with coffee spoons.' While I was in politics I measured out my life in coffee mornings. As my spiritual life began to take off I measured it out in prayer notebooks.

Keeping a prayer notebook, or diary, is a chore at the time but a joy afterwards. It is also a great strengthener of faith to turn back the pages years later and to see how many of one's prayer requests have been answered, although not necessarily in the way or time-scale originally asked for. However, at the time when the notebook is being written, one immediate blessing is the noting down of appropriate Bible passages as well as prayers by authors ranging from 1st-century saints to 21st-century evangelists. The paths trodden by such masters of prayer are well worth following and I hope I have reaped from them a rich harvest of what Shakespeare called 'other men's flowers' when compiling the various sections of this book.

For all its strengths, the Adoration-Confession-Thanksgiving-Supplication formula has its omissions and weaknesses. Perhaps the most glaring omissions are prayers of contemplation. As these usually take place in silence it would be difficult to devote many pages to them in a book of this kind. However, as I mention in relation to the *Three Crucial Questions* prayer on page 118, some of my own deepest moments of discovery have come from going down the contemplative path. In particular the nine-day silent retreat I did on the Ignatian Spiritual Exercises under Father Gerard Hughes' direction in 1998 was another major turning point on my journey.

Prayer needs to be balanced between the inward swing of contemplation and the outward swing of action. In this context 'action' can include doing, serving or praying in accordance with God's will. For me, at this time, action meant preparing to go to prison, since I had already confirmed my intention to plead guilty to charges of perjury arising out of the *Guardian* libel action. So my most frequent prayer request was: 'Lord, help me to survive in prison.' It turned out to be a prayer well answered.

On the first morning of my prison sentence, 9th June 1999, I awoke at 5.30 a.m. and wondered how I would survive the coming day. HMP Belmarsh was notorious for being 'a tough nick' and it had lived up to its reputation on the night of my arrival with dozens of its inmates participating in an obscene chant on the theme of Let's Get Aitken Tomorrow. Among the noisiest vocalists in the chant were the neighbours on my wing landing. Occupying the cells immediately to the left and right of me were a couple of prisoners who seemed to have cast themselves in the role of cantors. For after helpfully identifying my precise location in their sing-song voices, they would shout a question such as: 'What shall we do to Aitken (or Aitken's private parts) tomorrow?' From the other three sides of the exercise yard came a thunder of unprintable responses.

Although my blood ran cold when I first heard these raucous exchanges, the combination of physical exhaustion, saying a prayer and reading a psalm[2] caused me to fall asleep before the shouting had run its course. But the memory of these menacing obscenities came back all too vividly as I began to think about the day ahead.

In contrast to the cacophony of the night before, the stillness of the morning after felt amazingly peaceful. Belmarsh was as quiet as a becalmed battleship. Its silence was strangely conducive to prayer. As I took in my immediate surroundings I remember thinking: 'Now I can see why monks down the centuries have found cells

1. See *Psalms for People Under Pressure*, page xii.

such good places to pray in.' For confronted with the stark reality of being shut inside a 12 x 8 ft concrete walled box, whose main features were iron bars, iron door, iron bed, chair, table and toilet, I realised that life could only be liveable in these claustrophobic surroundings if one's spiritual heart and mind were in the right place. So I turned to God and prayed.

Prayer discipline works. My brain might have been whirling in a thousand different directions but I settled down into the routine of the ACTS structure I had been using ever since the Alpha course of October 1997. For obvious reasons I remember those particular morning prayers well, as usual recording them in my diary.

First came Adoration. What could there be to adore in God's glory and creation from a cell in Belmarsh? A nanosecond after asking this silly question I looked up through the bars and saw the most wonderful cobalt blue sky with the first rays of matinal sunlight dancing like golden ballerinas across the grey rooftops of the adjacent cellblocks. One of the short adoration prayers I had learned came to mind: 'O God, be exalted above the heavens: let your glory shine over all the earth.'

Next came Confession. I began with a familiar plea: 'Search me, O God, and know my heart; try me and know my thoughts. Look well if there are any wrongful ways in me, and lead me in your way everlasting.' Usually this prayer, from Psalm 139, brings up sinful junk by the bucketful. On this day it produced nothing. This was absurd. Here was I on my first morning in prison and I couldn't think of anything to confess! Was I praying in the wrong way? Of course the sins for which I was being punished had long ago been confessed to God. But even so, the idea that the previous day had been a sinless one was ridiculous. So I redoubled my efforts to bring to mind my sins. Still nothing happened.

Then an interesting thought came along. Tuesday, 8th June, had been a day on which many people were praying for me. I knew this from the breakfast prayers the Alison group members and others such as Charles Colson had said for me before we set off from my home to the Old Bailey. I knew it from the letters I had received that morning from complete strangers, from old friends and even from a hand-delivered note sent round from Lambeth Palace by Archbishop George Carey. I knew it from looking up from the dock of Court No. 1 of the Old Bailey at the public gallery just before the judge passed sentence. There I saw Lord Longford, Father Norman Brown of Westminster Cathedral, and James Pringle, sitting in the front row. All three had their eyes closed so I guessed they were praying. Putting these various fragments together I began to wonder if the reason why I had nothing to confess was that throughout the previous day I had been protected and guided by the supernatural forces of prayer.

Then I turned to Thanksgiving. At first glance there might seem to be precious little to give thanks for if you are locked up in Britain's highest security prison on the first day of your sentence. Not so. For some reason I dredged up from my memory William Law's advice about gratitude to God:

> 'If anyone would tell you the shortest, surest way to all happiness they would tell you to make it a rule to thank and praise God for everything that happens to you. For it is certain that whatever seeming calamity befalls you, if you can thank and praise God for it you turn it into a blessing.'

These 17th-century words set me off on a count-your-blessings exercise. There was a huge list of things to thank God for: his love, his forgiveness, his gift of a new life in Christ, even his chastenings. There were all sorts of practical reasons for gratitude too. The judge's eighteen-month sentence had been fair. My friends and prayer partners were wonderful. My family's morale, and my own, had held up better than expected. One way and another, thanking God came easily.

Moving on to Supplication, or asking, my children's needs were the top priority, followed by a handful of people whose serious illness or other difficulties made their plights even worse than mine. I also prayed for peace with the Editor of the *Guardian* and other journalists. These supplications ended by praying over some verses from Psalm 91. This is a great plea for God's protection from enemies, something I badly needed in the light of the previous evening's chantings and threatenings.

My prayers were interrupted by shouts of 'Unlock! Everybody out!' This was the daily wake-up call to the inmates of Belmarsh from its prison officers as they came down the wings unlocking our cell doors and ordering us to stand on the landings for the morning roll call. As I stepped out of my cell I remembered that the noisiest vocalists of the night before had been my immediate neighbours to my right and left. So I literally trembled as I stood on the landing beside them until it emerged that their nocturnal hostility had changed into amiability.

'G'morning,' said one of them, ' 'ope you slept well. Sorry about last night. We were on the tackle [drugs]. Just lettin' off steam.'

'Yeah, nothing personal mate,' said the other. 'Let's 'ave a rosie together at association.' [A cup of tea at tea-break time.]

As my eyes started to become accustomed to the landscape of prison I was surprised by many more unexpected discoveries. The first was how young everyone seemed to be. The average age of a British prisoner is twenty-three. So Belmarsh, like other big London prisons, has many teenagers within its walls. My second observation was the extraordinary availability and common usage of drugs. The third was that beneath the surface of these outwardly macho young men lurked a lot of human vulnerability.

One aspect of this vulnerability appeared on the second day of my sentence when a young black prisoner came up to me and said: 'I've just had a letter from me brief, but I can't read it. Would you do us a favour and read it?'

The letter I read aloud was a threatened eviction notice from the Lambeth Council. After some discussion it emerged that the prisoner's brother could take care of it by paying off the arrears in instalments. 'OK, let's tell the council that,' said my new friend, whose name was Stokesey. 'But I can't write either. Could you write it for me?'

So I wrote an appropriate letter to the Lambeth Council and Stokesey signed it. He was so delighted that he skipped away holding the envelope above his head, declaring at the top of his voice: 'That MP geezer's got fantastic joined-up writing.'

This commercial for my graphological skills fell on the ears of a surprisingly receptive audience. For approximately one third of British prisoners are unable to read or write. They often conceal this vulnerability from each other but it is revealed in the literacy tests all prisoners have to take at the beginning of their sentences. So an older prisoner who is willing to volunteer for the role of an amanuensis soon becomes a useful member of the community. What I could never have predicted was that my usefulness would lead to the starting up of a prison prayer group.

During the early weeks of my sentence I did a lot of letter reading and writing. At first this was the cause of some humour. One day an old lag came up to me and said: 'Jonno, do you realise you is havin' a fantastic impact on the girls of Brixton. They can't believe the sudden improvement in the quality of their love letters.'

Whatever was or was not happening among the ladies of Brixton, I got quite a few signs and comments of appreciation from my fellow prisoners. One of them was an Irish burglar, unsurprisingly called Paddy. He invited me into his cell for coffee and made a little speech of thanks. 'On behalf of the lads I'd really like to thank you for all the letter writing you've done for us,' he began, 'and I'd like to give you a present to say how much we appreciate it. So you can have anything you like – free of charge – from me library.'

At this point Paddy dived underneath the left-hand side of his bed and brought up an amazing selection of hardcore porn magazines.

'No, thank you,' I said, obviously reverting to the persona of a pompous politician because Paddy took umbrage.

'Too good for you, eh?' he said with a bitter edge to his voice. Before I had time to reply, Paddy's fertile mind thought up an ingenious explanation for my refusal.

'Ooh … if it's boys you're after,' he said, now diving under the right-hand side of the bed and coming up with an alternative selection of hard porn pictures.

'No, no,' I said hurriedly. 'I used to like the first sort of magazines you showed me but these days I'm trying a different path in life.'

'So what kind of path would that be?' asked Paddy.

'Well, if you really want to know, it's the path of praying to Jesus and obeying his teachings,' I replied. 'It's a path that has changed my life.'

A long silence spread over us in that cell. It was eventually broken by Paddy who, in a slow voice, said the unexpected words: 'You know, I'd really like to try that path myself.'

Before I could respond, the floodgates opened within Paddy and he poured out a litany of woes describing all that was wrong with his present path of life. Much of his misery came from the kinds of complaints that are often heard in the world of freedom.

'There's no meaning to my life … my wife doesn't understand me … all I care about is money and, when I've got it, there's no point to it … my relationships keep going wrong … my life's just empty … totally unfulfilled.'

After much more in this vein Paddy ended by saying: 'Me Nan [grandmother] used to believe in Jesus and she really had something. I can see that you've got something. So I'd like to try that path myself. I really would.'

One of my self-imposed survival rules in prison was that I had resolved never to talk about religion. Before I went inside, an ex-prisoner had warned me that 'Jesus freaks sometimes get served up' [beaten up]. So I had kept my prayers for the privacy of my own cell, until this moment. Now I realised that I had to respond to Paddy. So it was my turn to create a long pause between us, until I finally said:

'Well Paddy, if you feel that way why don't we say a prayer together?' I had moved a long way since the days when I thought that praying out loud would be worse than going to the dentist without an anaesthetic.

And so we prayed. First night, second night, third night. Then Paddy, who had in him the qualities of a good recruiting sergeant, decided that our two-man prayer partnership needed to be expanded. So he went off recruiting and came back with two or three of his friends, then two or three more, and then still more. Before we knew where we were we had gathered together about twelve young men in a rather unusual prayer group – so unusual that it gave a new meaning to the Christian term 'a cell group'.

We started off in considerable embarrassment. 'How do we pray?' someone asked. Hesitantly I described the ACTS structure. By the time I had finished I thought no one had understood my explanation. Then a Nigerian prisoner leapt in with a passionate extempore prayer on why he adored the Lord Jesus. We were off and running.

Far from being the tutor of the group, I was its greater learner and beneficiary. Until my time in prison I had prayed from my lips. It was my fellow prisoners who taught me how to pray from the heart.

Their examples showed me how little of prayer is to do with the human activity of polishing up words and phrases which we think are appropriate for addressing God. What my prison prayer partners instinctively knew was that prayer is a supernatural activity in which we rely on God to enter our hearts, and to let our feelings rise up to him in words, occasionally in silences, which he inspires. In retrospect, it seems extraordinary that I should have had to get into a prison cell to learn these facts of prayer life.

Once I understood why my 'experienced' prayers were less powerful than the 'inexperienced' prayers of my fellow prisoners, a new impetus came to my prayer life. Take Confession. Saying it with your lips is not enough. Changing your life with your heart, away from what you have confessed, is an essential part of the process. As John the Baptist urged his followers: 'Show the fruits of your repentance' (Matthew 3:8). The conflicting forces of good and evil cause struggles in every human heart. As I participated in prayer with those who were struggling against, say, the inability to forgive, I became much harder on my own failures in this area. This particular problem was solved for me by the advice of a Benedictine monk whom I met when he was walking round the exercise yard of Belmarsh dispensing pastoral advice. I told him of the problem I was having over unforgiveness, particularly towards one or two journalists who persisted in writing complete fiction about me. 'Pray to receive the gift of forgiveness,' said the monk, 'and when you receive it, give the gift back towards those towards whom you feel unforgiving.' So I prayed, and weeks later it all happened just as the monk had said it would. My unwillingness-to-forgive problem rolled off my shoulders and has not troubled me again since.

One of the most difficult areas of supplication in our prison prayer group was drug addiction. The jails of Britain are awash with horse, charlie, coover, tackle, and a dozen other exotically-named derivatives of heroin and cocaine. The prices are low, the dealers are persistent and the flesh is weak. But in some cases prayer was an enormous help to young men who wanted to break their habit and stay clean. Most of them had done Narcotics Anonymous courses of one kind and another that referred to the need for the help of 'a higher power'. What does this phrase mean in the context of secular NA or AA courses? At least a Christian prayer group can answer the question by praying for the power of the Holy Spirit to come into a drug user's heart and transform our weak will so that it harmonises with God's will. Also the accountability factor in a group of prayer partners can be a huge support in weaning drug users off their habit.

Drugs were only one of the pressures that caused turbulence in the lives of the members of our prison prayer group. We all had family worries, relationship problems, temptations, character failures, special situations and a mass of other baggage to bring before God. 'And who the hell is God anyway?' one inmate asked aggressively. Some of the answers to this question can be found in scripture. We had a terrific discussion in the group one night about God as revealed in Psalm 139. Another line of answer can be supplied by the doctrine of the Trinity. Even after two years of study at an Oxford theological college I am not sure I can explain the concept of a threepersonned God. But I understood it when I listened to the prayers of my fellow prisoners. For some of these young men would address their prayers to God the Father, not least because they had never known who their earthly fathers were. However, they knew they wanted a paternal presence bringing support, stability, discipline and fatherly love to their lives. Others prayed to God the Son, because they knew they needed to relate to Jesus and what he offered – compassion, forgiveness, healing and a love for sinners. And others prayed for the power of the Holy Spirit to come in and transform their lives so that they turned away from crime, drugs, anger and other demons.

This journey of prayer in prison was a journey of change. It was spiritual life in the raw, stripping away much of my own protective defences, which had separated me from God and my neighbours in the past. I am not the best judge of how much it changed me. All I can say for sure is that I came to love God and to love my neighbours (not all of them instantly loveable people!) far more than I had ever done before. That gain from prayer life as a convict now seems far more fulfilling than the prizes of public life as a Cabinet Minister. So for that reason, although it amazes many people, I now say from the heart: 'Thank you God for sending me to prison.'

One last reflection on my prison prayer life: In the 57 years of my existence before being driven through the gates of HMP Belmarsh, I had enjoyed many interesting, exciting, happy experiences in a varied and crowded career. Yet none of them gave me as much excitement, joy and fulfilment as my experiences in prison of coming closer to God in solitary prayer and bringing others closer to him in group prayer.

These prison prayer experiences were so intense that I probably needed a period of decompression from them after my release in January 2000. Unless you are a full-time minister, spiritual counsellor or member of a religious order it is simply not possible to spend several hours each day praying, either alone or with other people. Nevertheless, on a reduced scale, my prayer disciplines continued after I re-entered the world of freedom. The Michael Alison group, which had continued to meet every Thursday morning for breakfast in my home while I was away, welcomed me back. Strengthened in its membership by Brian, a fellow Old Belmarshian, and David Christie, a fellow Old Etonian, these brothers helped me through a difficult period of readjustment.

The next big milestone on my journey of prayer was entering Wycliffe Hall, Oxford. I do not think I fully appreciated at the time quite what a big risk Wycliffe was taking in admitting me as a student. For I remained a high-profile, controversial and colourful target for the media, which continued to present me in a negative light. My journey of faith, parts of which I had attempted to describe in its pre-prison phase in an autobiography, *Pride and Perjury*, was greeted with much cynicism. To make matters worse, Wycliffe had admitted an ex-prisoner as a student in the previous academic year and the experiment had failed. At least that failure had been veiled in obscurity, but any comparable weaknesses by me would be guaranteed maximum publicity. So the college was nervous about its reputation and I was hesitant about committing myself to two years of full-time study there. With both sides fluttering in our respective dovecotes Michael Alison again showed his steel. After much prayer he put heart into me and backbone into the Wycliffe tutors. The result was that in October 2000 I became an Oxford University undergraduate for the second time in my life.

Reading theology at Wycliffe, 40 years on from reading law at Christ Church, was a very different Oxford experience. In some after-dinner speech I later described the culture change by saying: 'At Wycliffe, I rise soberly and early in the morning, saying "Good morning God". At Christ Church I used to fall out of bed with a hangover at around noon saying "Good God, morning!"'

Early-rising Wycliffe gave me two of the most enriching years of my life. Its academic standards were demanding but its community life was loving. Most of my fellow students were training to be ordained ministers in the Church of England or other overseas churches. I was one of a small handful of publicans and sinners reading theology for their own (in my case unknown) purposes. When asked to explain what I was doing at an Anglican theological college I would answer: 'Trying to get to know God better.'

If I succeeded in this objective it was not through passing examinations in New Testament Greek, Church History, Christian Doctrine and Biblical Knowledge of the Old and New Testaments. It was through prayer. For it was the prayer life of Wycliffe that carried me into new and enthralling spiritual territory.

The highlights of my week were the tutored fellowship group sessions and the student-only cell group meetings. My fellowship group was led jointly by the Principal of the College, Professor The Revd Dr

Alister McGrath and by The Revd Michael Green. From these two great scholars I learned to love God as he reveals himself through scripture. The primacy of the word is heavily emphasised in an evangelical seminary, but Wycliffe encourages its students to range widely and deeply into studying the lives and writings of past saints. So Alister McGrath encouraged me to read Augustine, Clement, Julian of Norwich, Lancelot Andrewes, Thomas à Kempis, Francis of Assisi, Martin Luther, William Law, John Calvin, Ignatius of Loyola, Thomas Merton, Dietrich Bonhoeffer and many others whose prayers appear in these pages. Michael Green took me out into the world on missions to all sorts of communities, national and international, training me and my Wycliffe classmates to put our newly acquired knowledge into practice as student evangelists. Prayer was central to this mission work, as it was in the daily life of the college in our cell groups and in our individual prayer partnerships.

Two individual prayer partners became very special to me during my two years at Oxford, possibly because they were older men with backgrounds and past careers to which I could easily relate.

The first of these was someone who had nothing to do with Wycliffe. He was Sir Andrew Green, who had retired from a distinguished diplomatic career to the Oxfordshire village of Deddington. Our paths had previously crossed in Whitehall and in British Embassies abroad. Somehow we reconnected and became aware that we were again travelling on similar paths – this time of Christian searching. We began meeting and praying together on a regular basis. I credit Andrew with keeping me 'earthed' in the real world at a time when, without his intellectual and practical companionship in prayer, I might have become over-religious and taken myself too seriously in matters spiritual about which I still know far too little. Andrew may credit me with giving him prayer support when he was founding Migrationwatch UK, a now famous think-tank that monitors Britain's elusive immigration statistics. I know that Andrew's work for Migrationwatch is deeply rooted in his Christian faith and spiritual integrity.

My second individual prayer partner was fellow Wycliffe student Paul Zaphiriou, whom I had first met on the Alpha Course at Holy Trinity, Brompton, in 1997. Then he was a successful businessman. Now he is a Church of England clergyman at St George the Martyr in Holborn, London. He opened my eyes to his earlier spiritual heritage in the Orthodox Church, and it is his influence that has led

me to some of the Eastern prayers in this book. Paul and I have trav-
elled far together. Among our many bonds was the fact that having
arrived at Wycliffe as rather lonely and divorced middle-aged men,
both of us found love and are now happily married.

For me, marriage was a huge leap of prayer and faith, as well as
of love. The sad divorce from my first wife, Lolicia, in 1998 (entirely
my fault) had left me bruised. I resolved to stay celibate. For over
five years, with one brief lapse, this resolution prevailed. Then by a
series of coincidences Elizabeth Harris, with whom I had been
romantically involved 25 years earlier, re-entered my life. After a
number of chaste dinners and theatre-outings together we knew we
were falling in love.

When I started to tell my Christian friends that I was thinking
of getting married again to Elizabeth their reactions were mixed. It
did not help matters when the paparazzi began taking an interest in
us. Gossip column coverage with colourful references to Elizabeth's
former film-star husbands, Rex Harrison and Richard Harris, produced pained letters from Christian well-wishers, some of which
read more like the correspondence of ill-wishers. Elizabeth became
unsettled, particularly after a visit to a big evangelical church in
North Oxford, St Andrew's, Linton Road, where my talk was followed by some sanctimonious questions about our relationship.

Such hostility was upsetting but it was more than balanced by
the tender loving care of my closest prayer partners. Their main con-
cern seemed to be: Would Elizabeth be a supportive companion on
my spiritual journey? Would we be partners in prayer as well as in
marriage?

Although I felt sure the answer was yes, I committed the questions
to prayer, not least with Elizabeth herself. We became regular
churchgoers at St Matthew's, Westminster, whose sensitive and sympathetic vicar, Father Philip Chester, was a tower of support to us.
He married us in St Matthew's in June 2003. Elizabeth's faith is more
private but just as committed as my own. We now pray together every
night of our lives. As the dedication to this book says, she is my nearest, dearest and closest prayer partner. I thank God daily for her.

One development in my prayer life for which Elizabeth is respon-
sible is that I now enlarge the ACTS structure into the longer
acronym, ACTORS. The additional letters, OR, stand for 'Our
Relationship' which means our relationship with God. I have learned
on my journey that whatever life's pressures may be, a committed

relationship with God in prayer is the answer to all of them. As this relationship is constantly developing it seems appropriate to have a separate category of prayer under this heading, hence the section *Prayers For Our Relationship With God* in this book.

Although my journey of prayer has been a momentous one across extraordinarily varied scenes and settings, this introduction must end on a note of humility. For the journey is far from over. All I really know is how little I know about this vast subject. So I am extremely cautious about making suggestions to other people on how to organise their prayer life when I have so much to learn about my own.

We are all learners in prayer. Novices can often be better at it than so-called experts. God's ear is tuned to all voices and ways of praying to him. So we should pray as we can, not as how this or any other book tells us to.

That said, some paths of prayer signposted in these pages are well-tried and true. Travellers along such paths may be a much larger multitude than the statistics of religion suggest. For, interestingly, the opinion polls tell us that although less than 10 per cent of the people in contemporary Britain go to church, over 90 per cent of them say a prayer from time to time. The practice of prayer is far greater than the practising of religion.

Since direct communication with God in prayer is surely the truest path for a spiritual journey, my final prayer is that this small book may help others along that path and be for the greater glory of God.

PART II

Prayers of Adoration

1. King David's Prayer of Adoration
2. Psalm 95
3. Short Prayers of Adoration
4. A Prayer in Adoration of the
   Creator of the Universe
5. Two Hymns of Adoration
6. Prayers for Starting the Day
7. Set Our Hearts on Fire

King David's Prayer of Adoration

Praise be to you O Lord, God of our father Israel, from everlasting to everlasting.

Yours, O Lord, is the greatness, the power, the glory and the splendour for everything in heaven and in earth is yours.

Yours O Lord, is the Kingdom; you are exalted as head over all. Wealth and honour come from you; you are the ruler of all things. In your hands are strength and power to exalt and to give strength to all.

Now, O God, we give you thanks and praise your glorious name.

1 Chronicles 29:10–13

REFLECTION

This is one of the most magnificent prayers of adoration in the Old Testament. Its author, King David, was coming to the end of his long reign over Israel. The struggle for the succession to the throne among his sons had been fraught with feuds and rebellions. Eventually Solomon was chosen to be heir apparent, but the ageing David had to work hard to get this succession accepted by all the tribes. So he called together a great assembly of Israelite leaders, commanders, officers and officials on the eve of the anointing of Solomon by Zadok the priest. As both an appeal for unification and sanctification David composed this public prayer to Yahweh, the Lord God of Israel, with whom he had a deep personal relationship and in whose sovereignty he believed and trusted.

The prayer is a sublime example of David's literary and poetic skills. Its words of homage, recorded in 1 Chronicles 29:10–13, had the effect of unifying the monarchy and the people of Israel in adoration to the God of all greatness, power and glory. *Everything in heaven and in earth is yours*, is one of its majestic phrases – phrases which are as valuable in our private prayers as they are powerful in public occasions of worship.

Although first delivered on an eve-of-coronation state occasion in ancient Jerusalem over 2000 years ago, the prayer is still in use today in many liturgies.

When I hear or say David's prayer I like to think of the unbroken line of adoration which runs from ancient Israel to our 21st-century world, honouring the God who reigns *from everlasting to everlasting*.

Psalm 95

O come let us sing unto the Lord; let us heartily rejoice in the rock of our salvation.

Let us come before him with thanksgiving and show ourselves glad in him with psalms.

For the Lord is a great God; and a great King above all gods.

In his hand are all the corners of the earth: and the strength of the hills is his also.

The sea is his and he made it: and his hands created the dry land.

O come let us worship and fall down; and kneel before the Lord our maker.

For he is the Lord our God; and we are the people of his pasture and the sheep of his hand.

Amen.

REFLECTION

This great prayer of praise and adoration comes from the first six verses of Psalm 95. It has been used in daily worship for many centuries by both the Eastern and Western churches. In the 4th century Athanasius described its practice by the early Church of Constantinople: 'Before the beginning of their prayers Christians exhort one another in the words of this psalm.' This ancient usage spread across the world and to this day Psalm 95 is central to the traditional Catholic, Anglican and Orthodox services of Morning Prayer.

I often say this psalm at the beginning of my quiet time. It is a prayer that takes me into a mood of rejoicing, thanking and worshipping God for all his blessings. These blessings include being the rock of our salvation, the ruler of all the corners of the earth, the creator of land and sea and simply Our God.

The joyful acclamation of praise at the beginning of the prayer is tempered towards its end by a deeper note of holy reverence as we are commanded to *worship and fall down; and kneel before the Lord our maker*. The final sentence of the prayer is a reminder that the magnificent, omnipotent deity we have been praising is also a personal God who protects us, guides us and loves us. The gentle words, *we are the people of his pasture and the sheep of his hand*, create an image that is both paternal and pastoral. So although on one level this prayer is, in the words of King Henry VIII, 'a strong stirring to the praise of God', it also invokes our personal relationship with our creator. The combination of majesty and intimacy makes these verses of Psalm 95 a wonderful private prayer of adoration.

Short Prayers of Adoration

Be exalted O God above the heavens; let your glory shine over all the earth.
Psalm 57:13

Now to the King of the ages, immortal, invisible the only God, be honour and glory for ever and ever.

Amen.
1 Timothy 1: 17

O God my joy, my glory and my confidence.

Highest, best, most mighty; most far and yet most near; fairest and yet strongest; fixed yet incomprehensible; unchanging yet the author of all change; never new, never old;

O Lord I love thee!
Augustine, Confessions

To him who is able to keep us from falling and to present us before his glorious presence without fault and with great joy; to the only God our Saviour be glory and majesty, dominion and power now and for evermore.

Amen.
Jude 24

REFLECTION

Adoration is the starter motor of prayer. Without the honouring of God's presence by offering some preliminary words of adoration to him it is harder to set off in the right mood to other parts of the prayer map.

So as we turn the key to start the engine of our prayers we should remember that adoration is devoted to the glory of God. Our own concerns and petitions come later. The first phase of prayer should focus with awe and wonder on the transcendent and omnipotent presence of God.

Putting such homage into words is not easy. Although DIY prayer-givers can and sometimes should create their own offerings of adoration, there is much to be said for using familiar verses of scripture or the great sayings of saints to set the tone of the opening movement in our personal symphonies of prayer. One lesson to be learned from scripture and the saints is that brevity is the soul of adoration. God does not need flattery laid on with a trowel. He will surely be content with the simplest and shortest of honouring sentences if they come with reverence from an adoring heart.

In that spirit of honour and brevity I have chosen a few prayers of adoration which have resonated with believers down the ages. Having just advised against long-windedness I will avoid long commentaries on these selections. However, I do advise long pauses after the prayer of adoration has been said. The purpose of the pause is for building on the prayer to think glorious thoughts of God.

Holy, Holy, Holy is the Lord God Almighty. Heaven and earth are full of his glory. Glory be to you O Lord most high.   *Isaiah 6:3*

Blessing and honour and glory and power be unto him that sits upon the throne and unto the Lamb forever and ever.

Amen.   *Revelation 5:13*

Blessing and honour and thanksgiving and praise, more than we can utter, more than we can conceive be yours, holy and glorious Trinity, Father, Son and Holy Spirit by all angels, all men, all creatures for ever and ever.

Amen.   *Bishop Lancelot Andrewes*
(1555–1626)

O Lord, whom have I in heaven but you? And what is there on earth that I desire beside you?   *Psalm 73:25*

My God and my all!   *St Francis of Assisi*
(1181–1226)

To illustrate this practice, look at the first prayer, taken from Psalm 57: *Be exalted O God above the heavens; let your glory shine over all the earth.*

The imagination of the prayer-giver can reach wondrous heights as it seeks to use these words as a trampoline for soaring into a mood of adoration to God. Picture him on his throne reigning over the heavenly host. Reflect on his governance of the night sky with all its stars, which he made and calls by name. Ponder on his might, majesty, dominion and power over the universe. Rejoice in the beauty of his creation all around us here on earth. Thank him for loving this world so much that he sent his son to die on the cross so that we could be forgiven for our sins. Praise him for his mercy, his peace and his grace, that shine over us his children as we pray to him in faith.

Sometimes these glimpses of the glory of God are too huge for our mere mortal minds. In my own prayers of adoration I can soar too high. A good way to return to reality is to repeat a lovely verse by the psalmist of Psalm 139 who had the same problems: 'Such knowledge is too wonderful for me, too lofty for me to attain.' These words bring me back to earth as I move into the next phases of my chosen prayer pattern of confession, thanksgiving and supplication. They are all the richer because of starting with adoration.

A Prayer in Adoration of the Creator of the Universe

He who made the Pleiades and Orion, who turns deep darkness into dawn and darkens the day into night; who calls for the waters of the sea and pours them over the face of the earth – the Lord is his name.

Amos 5:8

REFLECTION

These words of the Old Testament prophet Amos make a wonderful short prayer of adoration. It is often used by monks and nuns of various religious orders in their daily office of Morning Prayer. The first time I recall hearing it, and being overwhelmed with feelings of adoration, was in St Faith's, the small Benedictine chapel off the north transept of Westminster Abbey, whose prayer-soaked walls have welcomed early morning worshippers for many centuries.

There is something about the night sky ablaze with stars that can stimulate thoughts of God even in the most agnostic of hearts. I particularly like the story told in his best-selling autobiography, *Born Again*, of what happened when 21-year old Lieutenant Charles Colson USMC gazed up at a starry sky from the deck of his warship, the USS Melette, as it was steaming towards combat:

'That night I suddenly became as certain as I had ever been about anything in my life, that out there, in that starlit beyond, was God,' wrote Colson. 'I was convinced that he ruled over the universe, that to him there were no mysteries, that somehow he kept it miraculously in order. In my own fumbling way I prayed knowing that he was there ...'

Perhaps such godly ponderings have captivated human hearts and minds ever since the time of the Book of Genesis where we are told simply, 'He made the stars' (Genesis 1:16). In our time the world's great scientific brains have reached a consensus that the universe was created by the 'big bang'. But who created the big bang along with the Pleiades, Orion, the waters of the sea, day and night? The scientists don't know. 'The Lord is his name', say faithful believers in this biblical prayer of adoration.

Two Hymns of Adoration

O worship the Lord in the beauty of holiness
Bow down before him, his glory proclaim
With gold of obedience and incense of lowliness
Kneel and adore him; the Lord is his name!

J. S. B. Monsell
(1811–1875)

Praise to the Lord! O let all that is in me adore him!
All that has life and breath, come now with
praises before him!
Let the Amen
Sound from his people again
Gladly for ay we adore him.

J. Neander
(1650–1680)

REFLECTION

When we turn to God with prayers of adoration we often grope for words with which to express ourselves. These two verses from well-known hymns fill that gap. Both contain glorious riches of praise.

O worship the Lord in the beauty of holiness is an opening line that sends hearts soaring to heaven. Yet simultaneously we are commanded to bow down and kneel. The exhilaration of worship is therefore balanced by a reminder to be humble and obedient before God. The mystic meaning of the gifts of the three wise men in their adoration to the baby Jesus is beautifully captured in the *gold of obedience and incense of lowliness* line. The climax of the verse, *The Lord is his name!*, has echoes of the first Christian believers who, in the days of the early church, proclaimed the entry of the Holy Spirit into their lives, with the cry 'Jesus is Lord!' as they entered the waters of baptism (1 Corinthians 12:3).

The second hymn of adoration is less mystical and more communal. There is something of the celestial cheerleader spirit in these lines. No living creature is left unreached by the exhortation: *All that has life and breath come now with praises before him.* After we made the welkin ring with *Let the Amen!* one sunny morning in a packed Wycliffe Hall chapel I remember a Welsh ordinand saying: 'The crowd at Cardiff Arms Park couldn't have done it better!'

Both hymns proclaim joy unconfined. Singing or saying these verses as prayers or adoration gives godly lift-off to the beginning of the day.

Prayers for Starting the Day

The Collect For Grace

O Lord our heavenly Father, almighty and everlasting God, who has safely brought us to the beginning of this day, defend us in the same with thy mighty power, and grant that this day we fall into no sin, neither run into any kind of danger but that all our doings may be ordered by thy governance, to do always that is righteous in thy sight, through Jesus Christ our Lord. Amen.

Book of Common Prayer 1662

The Gift Of A New Day

We give you hearty thanks O God for the rest of the past night and for the gift of a new day. Grant that we may pass its hours taking many opportunities for pleasing you, so that at eventide we may again give thanks to you, our Lord and Saviour Jesus Christ. Amen.

Daybreak Office of the Eastern Church, 3rd century

Set Our Hearts On Fire

As we rejoice in the gift of this new day, so may the light of your presence O God set our hearts on fire with love for you, now and forever, through Jesus Christ our Lord. Amen.

The Daily Office, circa 10th century

Chase Away Gloomy Thoughts

O God who has folded back the mantle of the night to clothe us in the golden glory of the day, chase from our hearts all gloomy thoughts and make us glad with the brightness of hope, that we may effectively aspire to unwon virtues, through Jesus Christ our Lord. Amen.

Gregorian Sacramentary, 6th century

Guiding To Eternity

O God who brought me from the rest of last night into the joyful light of this new morning. Bring me also from the light of the day into the guiding light of eternity. Through Jesus Christ our Lord. Amen.

Traditional (Gaelic)

REFLECTION

These prayers are all good day starters. I like to use one or two of them after having opened my quiet time with a more general prayer or psalm of adoration. It seems a logical sequence to move from glorifying the eternal presence and majesty of God into the time frame of a new morning with a more specific prayer relating to the day ahead.

These ten prayers are a personal selection. For example I love the opening prayer known to Anglicans as the Collect for Grace because it was read at every school and church service of Morning Prayer throughout my formative years. Now I try to reflect on its powerful phrases instead of letting them rattle into one ear and come out of the other without a thought.

Although the Collect for Grace is over 400 years old it is a mere stripling compared to my next five selections from Eastern, Gregorian, Catholic, Gaelic and other traditional morning liturgies. Some of these date back to the eras of the early and mediaeval church but their words seem as fresh as ever, which may be why they have survived across the centuries.

If one is starting the day in a downbeat mood of gloom then try the 6th century Gregorian prayer: O *God who has folded back the mantle of the night to clothe us in the golden glory of the day, cleanse from our hearts all gloomy thoughts and make us glad with the brightness of hope* ...

Devoutly, Busily And Merrily
Help us this day O God to serve thee devoutly and the world busily. May we do our work wisely, go to meat appetitely, sit thereat discreetly, arise temperately, please our friends duly, go to bed merrily and sleep surely – all in the joy of our Lord and Saviour Jesus Christ. Amen.   *Traditional, Middle Ages*

A Prayer At Coffee Time
Somehow Jesus, I like praying with a cup of coffee in my hands. I guess the warmth of the cup settles me and speaks with the warmth of your love. I hold the cup against my cheek and listen, hushed and still.

I blow on the coffee and drink. O Spirit of God, blow across my little life and let me drink in your great life. Amen.
                                       Richard J. Foster, Prayers from the Heart

Coffee With God
Heavenly Father, I thank you for this new day; for the sunlight streaming through the bars of my cell; for the taste of this warm coffee; and for your presence as you hear my morning prayers.

Lord as each day dawns I thank you for bringing me a step closer to freedom. Not just my physical freedom; far more importantly I thank you for the freedom of a new relationship with you.

Lord you have liberated me from the darkness of my past. Help me to stay faithful to you in the future – this day and on every day for the rest of my life. Through Jesus Christ our Lord. Amen.
                                                                                        J. A.

Dr Johnson's Prayer
O God, make us remember that every day is your gift and should be used according to your command. Through Jesus Christ our Lord. Amen.   *Dr Samuel Johnson (1709–1784)*

King Henry VI's Prayer
O Lord Jesus Christ, who hast made us, redeemed us, and brought us unto that which now we are. Thou knowest what thou wouldst do with us; deal with us according to thy will with mercy; for the sake of Jesus Christ our Lord. Amen.
                                                       King Henry VI (1421–1471)

Or, if you feel like a lighter note to brighten your morning, you may get a chuckle out of the traditional Middle Ages prayer (provenance unknown) that asks for God's help to *do our work wisely, go to meat appetitely, sit thereat discreetly, arise temperately, go to bed merrily and sleep surely*.

The two modern prayers that follow these ancient devotions both feature morning coffee. The author of *A Prayer at Coffee Time*, Richard Foster, adds this footnote: 'Often I will allow the coffee to determine the length of my prayer time. When the coffee is gone I am ready to turn my attention to the tasks of the day.' Rather an ingenious way of deciding the length of one's quiet time!

My own prayer, *Coffee with God*, was written in HMP Stanford Hill where I served most of my sentence for perjury. Because the main lights of the prison went out at 10 pm I was usually awake by 6 am. So I used to spend the first hour and a half before the morning roll call with a daily quiet time in my cell. My prayers were so much enhanced by cups of Nescafé mixed with powdered milk and hot water from the Heatrex machine adjacent to the spur showers that I came to call this fruitful period, 'Coffee with God'. It set me up with a framework of peace in which to endure the unpeaceful remainder of the day.

The selection ends first with a characteristically pithy prayer by the great Dr Samuel Johnson who was evidently as good at supplication to God in the morning as he was in conversation with Boswell in the evening.

Finally I conclude with King Henry's VI's prayer: *Thou knowest what thou would'st do with us; deal with us according to thy will with mercy*. I don't think I ever reflected on this Founders' Prayer when I heard it read every morning of my schooldays in Eton College Chapel. Now I think it is a beautiful daily reminder of the need to surrender our human will to the will of an omniscient and omnipotent God.

Set Our Hearts on Fire

Set our hearts on fire with love of thee O Christ our God; that in the flame we may love thee with all our hearts, with all our minds, with all our soul and with all our strength; and our neighbours as ourselves, so that keeping thy commandments we may glorify thee, the giver of all good gifts. Through Jesus Christ our Lord. Amen.

Eastern Orthodox Prayer

REFLECTION

To round off your morning prayers of adoration to a really rousing conclusion, how about asking God to *set your heart on fire*? The phrase is also used to describe recently converted Christians who are blazing away with enthusiasm for their new-found faith. This ancient prayer of the Eastern Orthodox Church is an encouragement to incendiary believers but also a reminder that their fire should be well earthed.

The prayer is earthed in the teachings of the Old and New Testaments. The exhortation to love God *with all our hearts, with all our minds, with all our soul and with all our strength*, comes from the Book of Deuteronomy which was written in about 1400 BC. These commands are known as the Shema (Deuteronomy 6:4–5). They became the foundation for the Jewish confession of faith, which to this day is recited in all prayers and services by the pious. Contrary to the spirit of the modern age, which is so prone to worshipping a multiplicity of false idols such as money, fame, celebrity or success, this prayer opens with a firm Shema-based plea to live a life centred on the one true God.

The prayer continues with reminders of Jesus' teachings: 'Love your neighbour as yourself' (Mark 12:21), and 'If you love me keep my commandments' (John 15:10). These and the demands of the Shema add up to a set of awesome commitments. Keeping them requires more than being *on fire*. The love, discipline and dedication needed to honour these commandments are spiritual gifts. We should ask to receive them, as this prayer does, from God *the giver of all good gifts*.

PART III

Prayers of Confession

1. A Prayer for God's Help as we Examine Our Consciences
2. A General Confession at Morning Prayer
3. A Prayer for Humility in Confession
4. King David's Prayer of Penitence
5. A Confession of Envy
6. Forgive our Foolish Ways
7. An Armenian Prayer for God's Mercy
8. The Denial and Repentance of Peter
9. A General Confession Before Taking Communion
10. Forgive Us for Spoiling Life at Home
11. No Excuses
12. Two Prayers for the Avoidance of Sin, by Søren Kierkegaard
13. A Prayer for Our Pain to Become Our Healing
14. The Paradox of Repentance
15. Two Prayers for Forgiveness, by John Donne
16. The Jesus Prayer
17. The Prayer of Commitment

A Prayer for God's Help as we Examine Our Consciences

Search me O God and know my heart, try me and know my thoughts. Look well if there are any wrongful ways in me and lead me in your way everlasting.

Psalm 139:23–24

REFLECTION

These verses from Psalm 139 are a good introduction to prayers of confession. For they open the door of our hearts to the cleansing process of calling to mind our sins, not just as we remember them but as God knows them.

Having our hearts searched by an omniscient God is a testing experience. Many of us are not particularly thorough self-searchers. We tend to edit out our failings or register them only in terms of external behaviour. The visible or audible sins we commit with our lips or in our lives need to be recorded in confession. But God goes deeper. He looks into the secret sins of our hearts, which may include jealousy, bitterness, envy, unwillingness to forgive, hypocrisy or pride. Perhaps God regards these as more important than the external sins we put at the top of our confession agendas. So it is good to ask for God's help when we examine our consciences using the opening words: *Search me O God and know my heart*...

I first came across this prayer in my prison cell while reading a book on the psalms by C. H. Spurgeon. On his advice, I have used it in my daily quiet time ever since. Its words operate like a divine dredging machine bringing up sins that I had forgotten about or glossed over.

The prayer does not leave us wallowing around in whatever it has helped us to dredge up. For its last six words, *lead me in your way everlasting*, are an appeal for God to set us on the right road of a life pleasing to him. That journey is bound to include many more stumbles, but this prayer can be a great help in keeping us on the straight and narrow path to grace.

A General Confession at Morning Prayer

Almighty and most merciful Father,
We have erred and strayed from thy ways like lost sheep,
We have followed too much the devices and desires of our own
    hearts,
We have offended against thy holy laws,
We have left undone those things which we ought to have done,
And we have done those things which we ought not to have done,
And there is no health in us;
But thou, O Lord, have mercy upon us miserable offenders;
Spare thou them, O God, which confess their faults,
Restore thou them that are penitent,
According to thy promises declared unto mankind in Christ Jesu
    our Lord;
And grant, O most merciful Father, for his sake,
That we may hereafter live a godly, righteous and sober life,
To the glory of thy holy Name.

Amen.

REFLECTION

This is the Church of England's general confession taken from the old service of Matins in the Book of Common Prayer. In short sentences intended to be read by the whole congregation it covers a huge horizon of sinfulness with phrases that a penitent heart will instantly translate from the general to the particular.

Other liturgies speak of sins of omission and commission. But no-one has ever divided these categories more eloquently than the author of this prayer with the words: *We have left undone those things which we ought to have done; And we have done those things which we ought not to have done; And there is no health in us.*

Halfway through this general confession there is a change of gear to a general exhortation addressed to God: *Spare thou them O God which confess their faults*, is the prayer's request. *Restore thou them that are penitent, according to thy promises declared unto mankind.*

What are these promises? They appear all over the New Testament but one of the neatest summaries of them is contained in these two verses from the first epistle of St John:

> 'If we say that we have no sin we deceive ourselves and the truth is not in us: but if we confess our sins he is faithful and just to forgive us our sins and to cleanse us from all unrighteousness' (1 John 1:8–9).

The problem with general confessions is that they can trip off the tongue at high speed but with low impact on our lives. At least the language here, and even more so in Archbishop Cranmer's general confession written for the service of Holy Communion (see page 60), is so powerful that it should make us stop and think about those devices and desires of our own hearts. The real test, however, is will we stop and change them?

A Prayer for Humility in Confession

O Lord, help us to avoid the proud speaking of the Pharisee and to learn humility from the sighs of the Publican as we cry out to you 'Lord have mercy on me a sinner'. In the name of the one who alone stands ready to forgive us. Our Saviour and Redeemer Jesus Christ. Amen.   *Eastern Orthodox Church*

REFLECTION

When we confess our sins we should pray to God with humble and contrite hearts. This is obvious but lots of people don't do it. As I used to be one of them I try to keep in mind this Eastern Orthodox prayer and the parable of the Pharisee and the Publican (Luke 18:9–14) on which it is based. They are important signposts for the right and wrong ways to pray.

Pride, wrote C. S. Lewis, is 'the complete anti-God state of mind'. Spiritual pride can be the most insidious demon of all. When we start to be proud of our piety or to believe that our religious virtues are earning us brownie points in heaven we are making a huge mistake.

Jesus pointed this out with humour in his caricature of the Pharisee in the parable. As a type this Pharisee is still to be found in many modern congregations. In contemporary parlance we might call him a 'Show Christian' or even a 'Sunday Christian'. That means someone who goes to church for external reasons such as wanting to give the appearance of being virtuous or religious.

God is uninterested in our external appearances. He looks at the internal depths of our hearts. If we are committed to genuine repentance our humility will be as clear as that of the Publican who stood at a distance. He would not even look up but beat his breast and said, 'Lord have mercy on me a sinner' (Luke 18:13).

The prayer ends up reminding us that although the Publican or tax collector stood at a distance, Jesus stood ready to forgive him. The connection between humility and forgiveness is well made. Proud speaking makes it impossible to tap into that connection. That is why we should pray to avoid the mistake of the Pharisee.

King David's Prayer of Penitence

O Lord have mercy on me according to your unfailing love and great compassion. Wash away all my iniquity and cleanse me from my sin.

Create in me a pure heart O Lord and renew a right spirit within me. Do not cast me from your presence or take your Holy Spirit from me. Restore to me the joy of your salvation and grant me a willing spirit to sustain me.

The sacrifices of God are a broken spirit; a broken and contrite heart of God you will not despise.

Psalm 51:1–4, 10–12, 17

REFLECTION

This great prayer of penitence, taken from Psalm 51, is a king's plea for forgiveness after an episode of terrible wickedness that included adultery, theft, conspiracy to murder, and murder.

King David's transgressions were appalling and he knew it. So the prayer opens with an abject cry for mercy. However, David also knew that nobody's sins are so bad that they put the transgressor below the reach of God's grace. The sacrifice of a broken and contrite heart is an offering that positions the sinner in a place where the gift of forgiveness can be received.

From its beginning in a deep mineshaft of guilt the prayer climbs a high mountain towards salvation. Cleansing, purification, renewal and restoration are passages on this journey. Empowerment comes from the Holy Spirit, a theological concept fully revealed in the New Testament. It makes its first and unexplained biblical appearance in this prayer. David, the Lord's anointed, evidently understood the transforming power of the Holy Spirit long before anyone else did for he prays that it will not be withdrawn from him.

The final sentence of the prayer contains two reminders. The first is that there can be no true penitence without pain. God sometimes has to chasten those whom he loves. David understood this and knew that he had to offer God his broken and contrite heart. The second reminder is that God never despises a penitent sinner. From Psalm 51 to the parable of the prodigal son, the biblical message is that God restores the joy of salvation to those who turn to him in contrition, penitence and faith.

A Confession of Envy

Lord, I perceive my soul deeply guilty of envy. Dispossess me of this bad spirit and turn my envy into holy emulation. Yea make other men's gifts to be mine by making me thankful to thee for them. Through Jesus Christ our Lord.

Amen.

Thomas Fuller
(1608–1661)

REFLECTION

Dispossess me of this bad spirit is a good prayer for those who are plagued by the green-eyed monsters of envy or jealousy. The 17th century historian, Thomas Fuller, who wrote it, evidently tortured himself with bitter feelings towards other writers. In a longer version of the prayer he says with anguish: 'I had rather my work were undone than done by another than myself!'

There's a lot of such jealousy about in our contemporary and highly competitive society. I have seen it in all walks of life, especially in politics at times of government reshuffles when Buggins gets promoted ahead of Muggins. Artists, actors and writers seem to be particularly prone to their strain of this unattractive disease. But I have even seen envy sprout among ordinands when one of their peer group was chosen to be curate in an interesting church. *This bad spirit* can turn up anywhere.

The first antidote to pressure from envy is to admit the sin to God. Thomas Fuller was well on his way to curing his fault because of the frankness with which he acknowledged it. Unfortunately it is more common for the envious to be in denial rather than in prayer about this secret sin of the heart.

Because envy and jealousy can be raging fires with a human soul they are difficult to extinguish. So after confessing the sin to God how do we stop committing it? Thomas Fuller offered an ingenious prayer suggestion. He asked God to make him thankful for the gifts of those whom he envied. By this gratitude to the source of all talent Fuller *made other men's gifts to be mine by making me thankful to thee for them*. Praying with God-centred thankfulness for someone else's talents is a great way of killing off the bad spirit of envy.

Forgive our Foolish Ways

Dear Lord and Father of mankind,
Forgive our foolish ways!
Reclothe us in our rightful mind,
In purer lives thy service find,
In deeper reverence praise.

In simple trust like theirs who heard
Beside the Syrian sea,
The gracious calling of the Lord,
Let us, like them without a word
Rise up and follow thee.

O Sabbath rest by Galilee!
O calm of hills above,
Where Jesus knelt to share with thee
The silence of eternity,
Interpreted by love!

Drop thy still dews of quietness,
Till all our strivings cease;
Take from our souls the strain and stress,
And let our ordered lives confess
The beauty of thy peace.

Breathe through the heat of our desire
Thy coolness and thy balm;
Let sense be dumb, let flesh retire;
Speak through the earthquake, wind and fire,
O still small voice of calm!

J. G. Whittier
(1819–1892)

REFLECTION

Although this poem by J. G. Whittier is better known as a hymn it also makes a wonderful private prayer. For three of its verses contain direct petitions to God expressed in such beautiful language that only a great poet could have composed them.

The *Forgive our foolish ways* verse is a prayer of penitence profoundly combined with the themes of redemption, purification, service and reverence.

The *Drop thy still dews of quietness* verse is a prayer for God's peace, which will give us ordered or obedient lives.

The *Breathe through the heat of our desire* verse is a request for our fevered desires to be cooled by God so that we can hear his voice above the noisy distractions and temptations of the world.

All three prayers have often resonated with me, sometimes at life's turning points. For example on our wedding day my wife Elizabeth and I chose to start the order of service for our marriage with the words of the first verse sung as a hymn. We both felt that asking to be forgiven our foolish ways of the past and to be guided towards purer lives of service in the future was a good start to our new life together.

The final verse is J. G. Whittier's poetic interpretation of that magnificent passage in the Old Testament in which the despairing Elijah flees to Mount Horeb after slaughtering the prophets of Baal (1 Kings 19). Elijah prays about his despair to God who puts on a pyrotechnic display of his power with earthquakes, wind and fire but speaks through none of them. Eventually he addresses his prophet in a *still small* voice as the King James Bible translates it. Perhaps we can only hear that voice when we have offered the first two prayers of penitence and peace and ceased our strivings against God.

An Armenian Prayer for God's Mercy

O Christ, Lord of Lords, have mercy upon me.
I beg you Saviour, have mercy upon me.
Wounded in sin, I fall down before you.
Do not overlook me. Have mercy upon me.

Sighing the tax collector received forgiveness in the
    Temple.
In his very words I too call out: 'Have mercy upon me'.

The thief on the cross cried out: 'Remember me Lord'.
In his very words I too call out: 'Have mercy upon me'.

Pleading, the Prodigal Son begged you:
'Father I have sinned against heaven and before you'.
In his very words I too call out: 'Have mercy upon me'.

Enlighten our hearts so that we may receive
The mercy that comes from you, O Lord of mercy
Lest like the rich man in the fiery furnace
We ask to be refreshed with a fingertip of water.
Hear us and have mercy on us O Christ.

You signified in the rich man and Lazarus
An example of the universal judgement
By handing them the contrary fates they received.

And so we ask you Lord
To save us from the fire of sin and suffering.
O Christ, Lord of Lords, have mercy upon us.

St Mesrob Mashtots
circa AD *410*

REFLECTION

This ancient Armenian prayer, composed in the 5th century and still regularly sung in the liturgy of that, provides powerful pictures of God's mercy and judgement.

The first three images of individuals who received the forgiveness of Christ, all taken from passages in Luke's Gospel, create a comforting portrayal of God's mercy. The tax collector in the temple (Luke 18:9–14); the thief on the cross (Luke 23:39–43) and the prodigal son (Luke 14:11–31) were utterly undeserving sinners. However, they repented and turned to God during their lifetimes and were rewarded with the gift of his grace.

The prayer ends with a different and disconcerting reminder, also from Luke's Gospel, that we will one day have to face God's judgement. We are warned that he may be a God of severity when judging those who have failed in their lifetimes to hear his word and to turn to him with repentance.

This warning is based on Jesus' story of the rich man and Lazarus (Luke 16:19–31). The rich man had lived a self-indulgent life, refusing to listen to the teachings of Scripture. So he received God's punishment – the torment of hell.

Most modern preachers avoid mentioning hell. Jesus, on the other hand, described it so vividly in this passage and in the Parable of the Sheep and the Goats (Matthew 25:31–46) that we would be well advised to take to heart these examples of what the prayer calls *the universal judgement*.

The repetitive rhythms of this Scripture-based prayer and the plea in the final stanza, *So we ask you Lord to save us from the fire of sin and suffering*, send a powerful, if uncomfortable, message. The Armenian Church makes a point in this prayer which most Western churches would rather not mention.

The Denial and Repentance of Peter

O Lord Jesus Christ, look upon us with those eyes of thine wherewith thou didst look upon Peter in the hall; that with Peter we may repent and, by thy same love be forgiven; for thine endless mercy's sake.

Amen.

Bishop Lancelot Andrewes
(1555–1626)

REFLECTION

This prayer is based on one of the most poignant moments in the passion of Christ. It is recorded in Luke 22:60–62 just after Peter has been asked for the third time in the hall outside the High Priest's house whether he is a companion of Jesus.

'Peter replied "Man I don't know what you're talking about". Just as he was speaking the cock crowed. The Lord turned and looked straight at Peter. Then Peter remembered the word the Lord had spoken to him, "Before the cock crows today you will disown me three times". And he went outside and wept bitterly.'

That look the Lord gave Peter was brilliantly captured in the Mel Gibson movie, *The Passion of the Christ*. But long before the power of the cinema focused on it, Luke's description of how Jesus 'turned and looked straight at Peter' captured hearts and consciences down the ages.

When Jesus turns and looks at us he knows all our secrets. His gaze will always be loving, sometimes reproachful. The challenge is in our response.

Bishop Lancelot Andrewes, who wrote this 17th-century prayer, knew how he wanted to respond. He asked to show the same repentance as Peter showed and to receive the same forgiveness that Jesus gave his flawed disciples. This was such full-hearted forgiveness that Peter became head of the early church. What an encouraging example of God's practice of taking the worst of sinners, forgiving them, changing them and using them in his service. Jesus' penetrating look can be the start of this divine process if we respond to it with true repentance.

A General Confession Before Taking Communion

Almighty God, Father of our Lord Jesus Christ, maker of all things, judge of all men: we acknowledge and bewail our manifold sins and wickedness, which we from time to time most grievously have committed, by thought, word, and deed, against thy Divine Majesty, provoking most justly thy wrath and indignation against us. We do earnestly repent, and are heartily sorry for these our misdoings; the remembrance of them is grievous unto us; the burden of them is intolerable. Have mercy upon us, have mercy upon us, most merciful Father; for thy Son our Lord Jesus Christ's sake, forgive us all that is past; and grant that we may all hereafter serve and please thee in newness of life, to the honour and glory of thy name; through Jesus Christ our Lord.

Amen.

Book of Common Prayer
Thomas Cranmer (1489–1556)

REFLECTION

This general confession from the Communion service in the Book of Common Prayer is a masterpiece of theology, spirituality and language. Composed by Archbishop Thomas Cranmer, it opens with a majestic definition of God, moves to a humble portrayal of penitence, offers an impassioned plea for mercy and closes with a fervent promise of service, obedience and newness of life.

Despite one or two anachronistic words, the cadences of Cranmer's powerful 17th-century prose flow magnificently. Only a cold and godless soul could fail to be stirred by the triple repetition: *Have mercy upon us, have mercy upon us, most merciful Father.* Only the most unrepentant of sinners could be left unmoved by the prayer's crescendo: *And grant that we may ever hereafter serve and please thee in newness of life, to the honour and glory of thy name; through Jesus Christ our Lord. Amen.*

As a 16-year old schoolboy I first became familiar with Cranmer's general confession when I was made to learn it by heart while preparing for confirmation. Although memorising it seemed a chore at the time, I shall always be grateful to the school chaplain, The Revd R. E. Sadleir, who drilled it into me. For although it lay dormant in my mind and heart for some 40 years, when I turned to God in penitence at the height of my troubles these great words of confession filled me with awe and wonder.

As a prayer this confession is intended to stimulate our thoughts of repentance individually, even though it is said generally. In earlier times, an examination of conscience was expected of faithful believers before they attended the service of Holy Communion. If the saying of the confession during the service becomes a mere ritual unaccompanied by personal repentance we may miss the deep meaning of Cranmer's beautifully polished jewels of spiritual wisdom. We may even miss the gift of God's forgiveness.

Forgive Us for Spoiling Life at Home

Forgive us O Lord, for everything we have done that has spoiled our home life.

For the moodiness and irritability that has made us difficult to live with;

For the insensitivity that has made us careless of the feelings of others, forgive us O Lord.

When we think of ourselves and of the meanness and ugliness and weakness of our lives, we thank you for Jesus Christ our Saviour, who died on the cross so we could be forgiven.

O Lord, give us a true penitence for our sins.

Grant that at the foot of the cross we may lay down the burden of our sins and find them rolled away.

And so strengthen us by the Holy Spirit that in the days to come we may lead a home life more pleasing to you, our Lord and Saviour Jesus Christ.

Amen.

William Barclay
(1899–1978)

REFLECTION

We often behave worst to our nearest and dearest. Moodiness, irritability, insensitivity and selfishness are faults that we are apt to conceal from outsiders such as our bosses and colleagues at work. But when we get inside our own homes, sometimes in tiredness and frustration at the end of a long day, these sins can boil over. If they do they may spoil the atmosphere and damage our relationships with those whom we most love.

Perhaps the above paragraph is too pessimistic a description of our own domestic circumstances. Yet the pattern is a well-known one. That is why Professor William Barclay, the eminent theologian and biblical commentator, composed this unusual prayer. I think he hit a bull's eye. For which of us has never been moody, irritable, insensitive or selfish in the privacy of our own home? There is no distinction in God's eyes between sinning in private or sinning in public.

Important though it is for us to make amends for such sins within our family circle, it is even more important to get ourselves right with God. This prayer is as practical as it is pertinent. For in addition to asking forgiveness for spoiling life at home (a sin whose seriousness can be underestimated by the sinner) the last two sentences of the prayer suggest solutions. The first is that we should lay the burden of our sins at the foot of the cross in true penitence. The second is that we should pray to be empowered by the Holy Spirit to lead better lives at home.

In this context, the old saying, 'home is where the heart is', has a spiritual meaning. For if we bring before God a humble and contrite heart when we have sinned against our nearest and dearest, our cleaner hearts will create a happier home.

No Excuses

Almighty God, in asking your forgiveness I cannot claim a right to
be forgiven. I can only cast myself upon your unbounded love.
I can plead no extenuating circumstances.
I cannot plead the frailty of my nature
I cannot plead the force of the temptations I encounter.
I cannot plead the persuasions of others who lead me astray.
I can only say: For the sake of Jesus Christ our Lord.

Amen.   *John Baillie*
                                          (1886–1960)

REFLECTION

This is a true prayer of penitence. Its author well understood the importance of total surrender in confession to God. For if we come before him with excuses for our sins we are only half penitent, which is the spiritual equivalent of being half pregnant.

Self-justification is for a worldly audience. A heavenly God immediately sees through our feeble excuses to him. 'Enter not into judgement with your servant O Lord, for in your sight can no man living be justified,' advised the author of Psalm 143. A similar message is given in the New Testament: 'If we say that we have done no sin we deceive ourselves and the truth is not in us. But if we confess our sins God is faithful and just to forgive us our sins and to cleanse us from all unrighteousness' (1 John 1:8–9).

What is important about this prayer is the abject and unconditional character of the penitent. It brings to mind the sense of utter unworthiness expressed by Isaiah when he had his vision in the temple. 'Woe is me,' he cried, 'I am ruined. For I am a man of unclean lips.'

Isaiah's contrition about his unclean lips was one of the signposts that guided me into pleading guilty to charges of perjury. Another was the third sentence of this prayer; *I can plead no extenuating circumstances*. Reminders like these helped me to realise that self-serving explanations to God for our sins are a waste of space.

The prayer reminds us that forgiveness is a divine gift, not a human right. However, the *cri de cœur*, *I can only cast myself upon your unbounded love*, will always get a loving response from the God who longs to forgive those who turn to him in true and faithful penitence.

Two Prayers for the Avoidance of Sin
by Søren Kierkegaard

[1]

Father in Heaven! Hold not our sins up against us but hold us up against our sins so that the thought of you when it wakens in our soul, and each time it wakens, should not remind us of what we have committed but of what you did forgive, not of how we went astray but of how you did save us!

Amen.

[2]

Lord, make our hearts your temple in which you live. Grant that every impure thought, every earthly desire might be like the idol Dagon – each morning broken at the feet of the Ark of the Covenant. Teach us to master flesh and blood so that this mastery of ourselves may be our sacrifice in order that we might be able to say with the Apostle 'I die daily'.

Amen.

Søren Kierkegaard

REFLECTION

If we are living in a personal relationship with God we will always be trying to please him. This means a constant struggle against the temptations of our sinful natures. How do we win that struggle? The message of these two prayers is that self-discipline is not enough. We need God's help and inspiration if we are to break our bad habits.

Søren Kierkegaard of Copenhagen, who wrote these prayers, believed that every individual must make his or her personal commitment to God. He attacked the comfortable institutional theology of the Danish State Church which minimised the importance of that individual commitment. So it is not surprising that both these prayers of Kierkegaard's are personalised recommendations on how to avoid sin.

The first prayer says, in effect, get so close to God that when you sin you immediately realise how much he is doing to forgive you and save you. Such a mind set is a powerful preventer of sin.

The second prayer is filled with the imagery of smashing our false gods of sin just as Dagon (the Philistines' god, the father of Baal) was mysteriously smashed every morning when the ark of the covenant (home of Israel's God Yahweh) was in the same temple.

Kierkegaard's idea is that if God dwells in our hearts he will break all the false gods such as sex or materialism that are in our temple. Mastering our impure thoughts and earthly desires so that we can dwell in God and he in us is a struggle. We can't do it on our own which is why the prayer begins: *Make our hearts your temple in which you live.* Doing it even with God's help means dying to sin on a constant basis. Hence the echo of St Paul's cry: 'I die daily' (1 Corinthians 15:31). A new life in Christ is both a joy and a continuous struggle.

A Prayer for Our Pain to Become Our Healing

May what comes to us in our time be for our healing in the ever-lasting years.

Amen.   *The Roman Missal*

REFLECTION

This prayer from the Roman Missal may be an encouragement to those who are enduring pain as a consequence of their sin.

I found it a source of such encouragement in the period after I had been caught out telling a lie on oath in a libel case. I was being flayed alive in the media. I knew the press campaign to have me prosecuted for perjury would succeed. All I could see ahead of me was the prospect of imprisonment, with all its grim consequences.

In the depths of this despair I received an unexpected letter from Robert Runcie, the retired Archbishop of Canterbury. He recommended this prayer. The more I pondered on it the more it comforted me.

What comes to us in our time can be interpreted as the temporary pains and punishment we have to endure after breaking our fellowship with God by sin. But if we accept those chastenings in penitence and faith as part of his plan for us we will be healed. Such healing may not come as quickly as we would like. God's timing is not our timing. But if we have the spiritual imagination to look ahead to eternity and believe that we will receive God's *healing in the everlasting years* there can be no greater blessing.

These thoughts have good collateral in scripture. Psalm 14:12–13 tells us, 'Blessed is the man you discipline O Lord ... you grant him relief from days of trouble'. Revelation 3:19 says, 'Those whom I love I rebuke and chasten. So be earnest and repent'.

However, none of these texts gives any guidance on timing. So we should not be over-confident that repentance will be a quick fix. However, we can be supremely confident that a loving God will give us his healing where it matters most. *In the everlasting years.*

The Paradox of Repentance

Lord ...
Thou hast brought me to the valley
where I live in the depths but see thee in
the heights, hemmed in by mountains of
sin I see thy glory.

Let me learn by paradox ...
that the way down is the way up
that to be low is to be high
that the broken heart is the healed heart
that the contrite spirit is the rejoicing spirit
that the repenting soul is the victorious soul
that to have nothing is to possess all
that to bear the cross is to wear the crown
that to give is to receive.

Let me find ...
thy light in my darkness
thy joy in my sorrow
thy grace in my sin
thy riches in my poverty
thy life in my death
... in no one else but thy Son, my Saviour, Jesus Christ.

Amen.

Anon.
from A Book of Prayers
(published by The Banner of Truth)

REFLECTION

This prayer was sent to me on the second day of my prison sentence in HMP Belmarsh by Jean Coats who later became a dear friend. Its words immediately spoke to me. They highlight a fascinating aspect of the God to whom we pray. In addition to all his other divine characteristics, he is a God of mystery and of paradox.

When Jesus came into this world through the mystery of the word made flesh, he was the fulfilment of many Messianic prophecies. But the people of Israel were expecting their long-awaited Messiah to arrive in pomp, glory and power. Instead of an omnipotent King they got a baby who was born in a borrowed manger; who grew up as a carpenter; who spent his time among the poor, the sinful, and the broken-hearted; who rode into Jerusalem on a borrowed donkey; who died in shame on the cross; and who was furtively buried in a borrowed tomb. These paradoxes seemed so unbelievable at the time that most people in 1st-century Palestine disbelieved and rejected Christ.

Godly paradoxes still abound in our 21st century world. If you are sitting in a prison cell it is difficult to swallow the claims made in the middle section of this prayer: *the way down is the way up … the broken heart is the healed heart … the repenting soul is the victorious soul.* A cynic will reject such possibilities. A believer will pray that God's paradoxical promises may come true.

In my life the promises did come true. Why? I think Martin Luther came as close as anyone to unlocking the paradoxical secret of an intimate relationship with God when he wrote: 'It is in our pain and in our brokenness that we can come closest to Christ.' Once that closeness is established, with God all things are possible.

Two Prayers for Forgiveness
by John Donne

[1]

Forgive me, Lord, my sins – the sins of my youth, the sins of the present; the sins I laid upon myself in an ill pleasure, the sins I cast upon others in an ill example; the sins which are manifest to all the world, the sins which I have laboured to hide from mine acquaintance, from mine own conscience, and even from my memory; my crying sins and my whispering sins, my ignorant sins and my wilful; sins against my superiors, equals, servants, against my lovers and benefactors, sins against myself, mine own body, mine own soul, sins against thee, O almighty Father, O merciful Son, O blessed Spirit of God. Forgive me, O Lord, through the merits of thine anointed, my Saviour, Jesus Christ.

Amen.

John Donne
(1573–1631)

REFLECTION

John Donne was a man of passion and of many parts. At various stages of his life he was a scholar, a satirist, a libertine, a military adventurer, a prisoner, a poet and a Church of England vicar (of Sevenoaks). His eloquent preaching brought him to the notice and favour of King James I, who said: 'London is a dish Dr Donne loves well. I shall carve for him a place at St Paul's.' That was how John Donne became Dean of St Paul's Cathedral in 1621. From its pulpit he built a huge following as a preacher until his death 10 years later.

The first of these prayers is a passionate recital of the many circumstances and categories of sin which Donne was bringing before God with a plea for his forgiveness. Whenever I read this prayer I am jolted into anxieties about the sins *which I have laboured to hide from mine acquaintance, from mine own conscience and even from my memory*. It is a reminder that suppressing or forgetting our sins will not fool God, however successfully we may fool ourselves.

I am also unsettled by *whispering sins* and *ignorant sins*. What are they? The first may have echoes of the saying, 'If you won't listen to God's whispers one day you'll have to listen to his shouts.' The second may refer to the sins we choose to ignore. It is better to lay them out before God in transparent penitence just as Donne was doing.

[2]

Wilt thou forgive that sin where I begun,
Which was my sin, though it were done before?
Wilt thou forgive that sin, through which I run,
And do run still: though still I do deplore?
When thou has done, thou has not done,
For I have more.

Wilt thou forgive that sin by which I have won
Others to sin, and made my sin their door?
Wilt thou forgive that sin which I did shun
A year, or two; but wallowed in, a score?
When thou has done, thou has not done,
For I have more.

I have a sin or fear, that when I've spun
My last thread, I shall perish on the shore;
Swear by thyself that at my death thy son
Shall shine, as he shines now, and heretofore;
And, having done that , thou hast done, I fear no more.

John Donne
(1573–1631)

This second prayer by John Donne was originally written as a hymn but it is so personal an address to God that it is perfect material for use in private confession. However I suspect that the gloomy forebodings expressed in these lines are overdone (no pun intended) possibly because Donne was going through one of his periodical bouts of ill heath. For he seems to be in a mood of excessive morbidity as he confesses his sins of the flesh and spirit with the refrain, *for I have more*. What *more* means in this context is the confession that he fears death – if it will result in him perishing on the shore of hell.

Such fear was surely unjustified from a great servant for God whose prayers and poems show him to have had the heart and humility of a true penitent. So Donne rightly recovers from his morbidity and ends these verses on a note of no fear or, rather, confidence in Jesus' promises of eternal life. The ending brings to mind the words of 1 John 4:18, 'Perfect love casts out fear'.

The Jesus Prayer

Lord Jesus Christ, Son of the Living God, have mercy upon me, a sinner.

REFLECTION

The Jesus Prayer is the most famous prayer of the Eastern Church and is becoming increasingly well known to Christians all over the world.

Dating back in its origins to the prayers of the Desert Fathers, the Jesus Prayer is sometimes known as the prayer of the heart, the prayer of silence, or the unceasing prayer. It is meant to be repeated over and over again in order to bring the prayer-giver to deeper levels of communion with God.

Although repetition of the Jesus Prayer is essential, this practice should not be 'vain repetition'. As Bishop Kallistos Ware has written in *The Orthodox Way*: 'The Jesus Prayer is not just an hypnotic incantation but a meaningful phrase, an invocation addressed to another person ... it should not be said mechanically but with inward purpose.'

One of the purposes of the prayer on which the Orthodox Church places great emphasis is *kenosis*, a Greek word meaning emptying which St Paul uses about Christ in his letter to the Philippians (Philippians 2:6–11). According to Eastern tradition the repetition of the Jesus Prayer empties our conscious minds of distractions, personal thoughts and worldly pressures. As these drain away we become subconsciously aware of a closeness to God's presence. This may bring us into deeper spiritual experiences such as meditation, contemplation and purification.

When I first heard about the Jesus prayer I am afraid I dismissed it as a step too far into Eastern mysticism. Perhaps I was not ready for it, being long on impatience and short on penitence. But sitting in a prison cell for seven months where I learned much about patience and my own need for repentance I gave the Jesus Prayer a serious try. The repetition seemed strange at first but, to cut a long story short, it worked. May it work for you too.

The Prayer Of Commitment

Lord Jesus Christ,

I am sorry for the things I have done wrong in my life [take a few moments to ask his forgiveness for anything particular that is on your conscience]. Please forgive me. I now turn from everything which I know is wrong.

Thank you that you died on the cross for me so that I could be forgiven and set free.

Thank you that you offer me forgiveness and the gift of your Spirit. I now receive that gift.

Please come into my life by your Holy Spirit to be with me forever.

Thank you, Lord Jesus.

Amen.

From Why Jesus *by the Revd Nicky Gumbel (born 1956)*

REFLECTION

This simple prayer is known as The Prayer of Commitment. It is central to the Alpha Course, an introductory course of talks and discussions on the Christian faith. Alpha has brought millions of people, including me, into a new relationship with Jesus Christ as a result of its teachings.

The Prayer of Commitment breaks down into three parts. The first paragraph is a prayer of repentance, confessing what is wrong in our lives and turning away from those sins. The second paragraph consists of saying 'thank you' to Jesus for dying for us on the cross and offering us his free gifts of forgiveness and a new life in him. The third paragraph is our invitation to Jesus to come into our lives.

Many have found the prayer a deeply moving turning point in their lives. Others may find it too simplistic. Both groups can agree that the greatest journeys begin with a single step. It is also common ground that a life is not made over to God by saying a few oral words of commitment. That happens as a result of the long, unremitting effort to stay faithful to God in the relationship which the Prayer of Commitment begins.

When I turned up to my first Alpha meeting I thought I did not need either the course or the Prayer of Commitment. God had other ideas. Why he decided to make it a turning point in my life is a mystery. But the Prayer of Commitment was a real call to a new relationship with him. Eight years later I can look back and say of this prayer: It was the beginning of a change to a new life in Christ.

PART IV

Prayers of Thanksgiving

1. A Call to Give Thanks
2. St Paul's Prayer of Thanksgiving for God's Grace
3. Two Prayers for a Grateful Heart
4. In Thanksgiving for Answered Prayer
5. General Thanksgiving

A Call To Give Thanks

If anyone would tell you the shortest, surest way to all happiness
they would tell you to make it a rule to thank and praise God for
everything that happens to you. For it is certain that whatever seem-
ing calamity befalls you, if you can thank and praise God for it you
turn it into a blessing.

William Law
(1616–1673)
from A Serious and Devout Call to a Holy Life

REFLECTION

Thanking God when things are going well for us is easy. Thanking him when we are being hit by life's misfortunes and calamities is extremely difficult. Is this prayer just hopelessly unrealistic?

When I was going through terrible problems a friend recommended that I should seek spiritual guidance from an elderly monk. When I met this venerable figure in his monastery he was hard of hearing so I had to raise my voice to summarise my problems, which at the time consisted of defeat, disgrace, divorce, bankruptcy and imminent jail. When I had finished this litany of woes the old monk lent forward and said in his quavery voice: 'Have you tried thanking God for them?'

Although thoroughly irritated at the time I now wished I had responded far more thoughtfully to the monk's question, which may well have been drawn from this famous spiritual advice from William Law. For although praying to God with thanks when our lives are going pear-shaped is an almost impossible challenge, we should ponder on the argument for trying to rise to it.

Surrendering to God's mysterious will and purpose is our duty and our joy if we truly believe in him. Whether we are being afflicted or blessed by his will we should thank him just the same. As Thomas à Kempis wrote in *The Imitation of Christ*: 'If thou wilt that I should be in the light blessed be thou. And if thou wilt that I be in the darkness blessed be thou. Light and darkness, life and death, praise ye the Lord.'

Perhaps one has to be as holy as Thomas à Kempis, William Law and other great men and women of God to follow this path of spiritual gratitude to the full. Yet attempting to do so may be a test to which we are called.

St Paul's Prayer of Thanksgiving for God's Grace

Blessed be the God and Father of Our Lord Jesus Christ, the Father
of all mercies and God of all comfort who comforts us in all our
troubles so that we can comfort those in any trouble with the comfort which we ourselves have received from God. For as we share
abundantly in Christ's suffering so through Christ we share abundantly in his comfort too.

2 Corinthians 1:3–5

REFLECTION

God is a compassionate and comforting God. He shares in our sufferings and grieves with us in our grief. It is right to thank him, as this prayer of St Paul does, for giving us his comfort in our times of trouble.

The five-fold repetition of the word *comfort* in this prayer might make it sound almost too comforting were it not for the pointed reference to Christ's sufferings. These change everything. They were first prophesised in the suffering servant passage of Isaiah, which described the unknown victim as 'despised and rejected; a man of sorrows and acquainted with grief... he was wounded for our transgressions, crushed for our iniquities, upon him was the punishment that made us whole and by his stripes we are healed' (Isaiah 53:3–5).

This passage, perhaps more powerfully than any other, captures the idea of the compassion of Christ. To know him is to understand that he died for our sins on the cruel cross of Calvary. He hung and suffered there for us, for you, for me.

Because of his sufferings on the cross, Jesus empathises with our contemporary sufferings. As a result, he offers us his comfort in our troubles, not as a spectator or even as a counsellor, but as a co-participant. The literal translation of the two Latin words from which compassion is derived (*cum* = with; *passio* = suffer) means suffering with. That is what makes Jesus' comfort so unique. Because he suffered for us he is with us in our sufferings. There are times when we should give thanks for this comforting and compassionate dimension of our relationship with God.

Two Prayers for a Grateful Heart

[1]

O Lord, thou hast given so much to me; give one thing more; a grateful heart.

Amen.

George Herbert
(1593–1633)

[2]

O Lord, that lends me life,
Lend me a heart replete with thankfulness.

William Shakespeare
(1564–1616)

REFLECTION

Two great poets share this simple prayer request. Perhaps their eminence will highlight its importance. For gratitude to God needs to be given a far higher priority than it gets in most people's prayers.

We are not so much ungrateful as forgetful when it comes to giving thanks to God. As in our relationship with our earthly parents we have a tendency, at least in Western society, to take for granted the provision of daily blessings such as food on the table, clothes on our backs or a roof over our heads. Perhaps it takes a spell of suffering in the deserts of deprivation before we realise the importance of thanking God for what we regard as normal in the pastures of plenty.

In the comfort zone of complacent spirituality it is equally easy to become unmindful of God's daily blessings. Dietrich Bonhoeffer argued that inadequate gratitude impedes spiritual growth. 'Only he who gives thanks for the little things receives the big things,' he wrote. 'We prevent God from giving us the great spiritual gifts he has in store for us because we do not give thanks for daily gifts.'

It's a provocative thought to which we can only respond from our hearts. If we start saying thank you to God by rote in the manner of an American checkout clerk in a supermarket repeating 'Have a nice day', such synthetic gratitude will be meaningless.

So George Herbert and William Shakespeare, contemporaries and literary geniuses in writing about the human condition, touched on a universal spiritual need in their respective prayer requests for a grateful or thankful heart.

In Thanksgiving for Answered Prayer

O God, thank you for hearing my prayer and granting my request.
Thank you for all the goodness, mercy and kindness you have shown
   me.
Thank you for your great love in giving me my life.
Thank you for your patience in forgiving me my sins.
Thank you for your protection in the past and for the opportunity
   to serve you in the future.
Thank you, Holy Spirit of God, for bestowing grace on my soul and
   for having renewed your life within me.
May my life from now on be a sign of my gratitude.

Amen.   *from* The Catholic Prayer Book 2003

REFLECTION

It is surprising how often we forget to thank God for answering our prayers. In the gospel story of the ten men healed by Jesus of leprosy only one of them (a Samaritan) came back to say thank you.

'Where are the other nine?' asked Jesus. 'Was no one found to return and give praise to God except this foreigner?' (Luke 17:18).

The nine out of ten failure rate is probably still about the average today. But in spiritual life, as in ordinary life, some people are much better at expressing gratitude than others. This prayer is a marvellous offering of thanks to God because it goes far wider and deeper than a thank-you for the original favour granted.

There are similarities in this Catholic prayer with the Anglican General Thanksgiving (see next page), which praises God 'for our creation, preservation, and for all the blessings of this life.' Here God is thanked more personally for *giving me life*, as well as for *forgiving me, bestowing grace on my soul* and for past protection. So great is the sense of thankfulness that an offer is made of future service to God as *a sign of my gratitude*.

God is sure to be pleased by such manifestations of thanks to him, not just for enormous blessings like being healed of leprosy but, just as importantly, for the small day-to-day benefits of life which are so easily taken for granted. We must beware of being ungracious to God. As Archbishop William Temple once warned: 'It is probable that in most of us the spiritual life is impoverished because we give so little place to gratitude. It is more important to thank God for blessings received than to pray for them beforehand.'

Saying this prayer on a regular basis is a right response to such warnings and a fine act of thanksgiving to God.

General Thanksgiving

Almighty God, Father of all mercies, we thine unworthy servants do give thee most humble and hearty thanks for all thy goodness and loving-kindness to us, and to all men.

We bless thee for our creation, preservation, and all the blessings of this life; but above all for thine inestimable love in the redemption of the world by our Lord Jesus Christ; for the means of grace, and for the hope of glory.

And, we beseech thee, give us that due sense of all thy mercies, that our hearts may be unfeignedly thankful, and that we show forth thy praise, not only with our lips, but in our lives; by giving up ourselves to thy service, and by walking before thee in holiness and righteousness all our days.

Through Jesus Christ our Lord, to whom with thee and the Holy Ghost be all honour and glory, world without end.

Amen.
from the Book of Common Prayer
ascribed to Bishop Reynolds
(1559–1676)

REFLECTION

The General Thanksgiving is one of the jewels of the 1662 Book of Common Prayer. Although rarely used nowadays because some of its language seems old-fashioned, it nevertheless contains beautiful thoughts and phrases which are perfect for expressing our gratitude to God.

The flowing cadences of this prayer are equal to the finest passages of Shakespeare, Milton, Cranmer and other masters of the English language. Bishop Reynolds wrote them for church congregations to say aloud together and this form of communal thanksgiving can still work magnificently with modern congregations.

I know this because at one group service during my two years of reading theology at Wycliffe Hall, Oxford we brought it to an end by saying together the General Thanksgiving. Despite a widespread unfamiliarity with the Book of Common Prayer, the effect of the General Thanksgiving was electrifying, possibly because we were saying it just after we had received our unexpectedly but universally successful exam results for Part I of the BTh! From the atmosphere in the chapel and from the comments around the college for days afterwards it was clear that these 16th-century words still had the power to move 21st-century hearts.

In churches, the General Thanksgiving is reserved for special occasions of gratitude in communal worship. Yet I have found it a marvellous mood setter in private prayer particularly when used on days of joy. I said it on the morning of my release from prison and on the morning of my marriage to Elizabeth. Life was full of blessings on both days, but the prayer's reminders of how God likes to be thanked for his mercies were important also. The General Thanksgiving is both a prayer of gratitude and a call to service.

PART V

Prayers for Our Relationship With God

1. Two Prayers of St Clement
2. A Prayer for the Cleansing of Our Hearts
3. A Prayer for the Royalty of Inward Happiness
4. A Prayer of Human Uncertainty and Godly Trust
5. A Prayer to Grow in Faith
6. Martin Luther's Prayer on Emptiness and Weakness of Faith
7. A Prayer to Stay Connected With God
8. A Prayer for Self Control
9. Shut Out Everything Except God
10. To Care Only for God's Approval
11. A Prayer for Perseverance
12. Augustine's Prayer for Purity of Heart
13. Three Crucial Questions
14. A Prayer for God's Mercy, Peace and Grace

Two Prayers of St Clement

[1]

Almighty God, Father of our Lord Jesus Christ,
grant, we pray, that we might be grounded
and settled in your truth by the coming
of your Holy Spirit into our hearts.

What we do not know, reveal to us;
What is lacking within us, make complete;
That which we do know, confirm in us;
And keep us blameless in your service,
through Jesus Christ our Lord.

Amen.

[2]

Lord, we beseech you to help and defend us.
Deliver the oppressed, pity the poor,
uplift those who have fallen,
be the portion of those in need,
return to your care those who have gone astray,
feed the hungry, strengthen the weak,
and break the chains of the prisoners.

May all people come to know that you only are God,
that Jesus Christ is your child,
and that we are your people and
the sheep of your pasture.

Clement, Bishop of Rome
(circa AD 95)

REFLECTION

These two prayers date back to the earliest days of the church. They were written by St Clement, a first century Christian martyr who has long interested me because for some years I worshipped At St Clement's Church, Sandwich, in my former constituency.

Christian tradition says that St Peter, Jesus' disciple, baptised Clement himself. Later in his life Clement became the third Bishop of Rome (from AD 88–97) after Peter and a man named Cletus. In AD 95 Clement wrote a pastoral letter to the Church of Corinth advising them on the need for harmony and unity among their believers. These two prayers come from that letter.

The prayer to be *grounded and settled in your truth by the coming of your Holy Spirit into our hearts* was a good plea for the new Christians in the Church of Corinth. It remains a good prayer for many new Christians today. As we know from St Paul's first letter to the Corinthians, they were an exuberant flock, claiming to possess all sorts of exciting spiritual gifts. Some of those claims may well have been genuine but as a congregation, the early Corinthians needed to be *grounded* and *settled* and to develop a sense of humility about their spiritual knowledge as well as a sense of decorum about their personal behaviour. To this day, some new Christians, exuberantly filled with the Holy Spirit after a heady conversion experience, can benefit from St Clement's words of wisdom. The message of them is that the Holy Spirit not only lifts us up; he also grounds us, settles us down in peace, reveals knowledge to us and keeps us blameless in your service.

The second prayer is an exemplary summary of faith in action. Based on Jesus' teachings they cannot be bettered as a short prayer of pastoral imperatives. Both these prayers of St Clement will help believers to deepen their relationship with God.

A Prayer for the Cleansing of Our Hearts

Almighty God, unto whom all hearts are open, all desires known, and from whom no secrets are hidden; cleanse the thoughts of our hearts by the inspiration of your Holy Spirit, that we may perfectly love you and worthily magnify your holy name, through Jesus Christ our Lord.

Amen.

REFLECTION

This is a much loved prayer, often called The Collect for Purity, because it is said at the beginning of the Anglican Communion serv- ice. However, it was in use by Gregorian monks at least a thousand years before Archbishop Cranmer put it into the Book of Common Prayer. The beauty and holiness of its words are timeless.

The three theological descriptions of God in the opening line of the prayer portray him in his love and in his omniscience. Because he loves us, he welcomes all who open our hearts to him. Because of his omniscience he knows all our desires and secrets. So often we approach God in prayer with acute anxiety about our sins and weak- nesses. But he knows them all anyway! Yet nothing pleases him more than a heart that opens up to him in penitence and faith.

The great line of the prayer is: *cleanse the thoughts of our hearts by the inspiration of your Holy Spirit.* This is a plea we need to make frequently. For our sinful natures will always be with us and we need them cleansed. However, we must not think of the Holy Spirit mere- ly as a celestial vacuum cleaner. He is infinitely more powerful.

This prayer recognises the nature of his transforming power by its use of the key word, *inspiration.* It does not ask for us to be cleansed, meaning scrubbed up. It asks for the thoughts of our hearts to be inspired, meaning lifted up.

We need the power of holy inspiration because of what the French mystic Abbé Huvelin called 'Our incurable mediocrity of soul'. Without the Holy Spirit we will never cure or cleanse our mediocre spiritual lives. With his power we can be transformed into souls who will *perfectly love you and worthily magnify your holy name.*

A Prayer for the Royalty of Inward Happiness

Grant unto us O Lord the royalty of inward happiness and the serenity which comes from living close to thee.

Daily renew in us the sense of joy and let thy Eternal Spirit dwell in our souls and bodies, filling every corner of our hearts with light and gladness. So that bearing about with us the infection of a good courage, we may be diffusers of life giving thee thanks always for all things.

Through Christ our Lord.

Amen.   *Anon.*
known as The Prayer of St Michael and St George

REFLECTION

This prayer is full of powerful and glorious phrases. Its anonymous author must have been a master of the English language. There are at least eight requests to God here, all expressed with originality and eloquence.

The Christian faith is centred on God's love and the qualities it gives to our hearts – joy, happiness, peace, gladness and gratitude. All are mentioned in this prayer, often in memorable words such as: the *royalty of inward happiness … the serenity which comes from living close to thee … filling every corner of our hearts with light and gladness*. Yet there are touches of steel in the prayer too. We are reminded that it is our duty to seek daily renewal of our faith, to thank God *always for all things* (including, no doubt, for life's difficult things), and to carry ourselves with *the infection of a good courage*. At the heart of the prayer is an appeal for the Holy Spirit to *dwell in our souls and bodies*. It ends with a request that *we may be diffusers of life*, which I interpret as spreaders or communicators of the Christian life and Gospel.

The Knights and Companions of St Michael and St George like to claim that this prayer belongs to their order and it is said regularly for them in their chapel at St Paul's Cathedral. Although an entirely appropriate prayer for a noble order of chivalry (these days consisting largely of Foreign Office diplomats), its origins are more ancient and its appeal is more universal. For any believer who is granted the requests in this prayer will surely have a close and good relationship with God.

A Prayer of Human Uncertainty and Godly Trust

My Lord God, I have no idea where I am going. I do not see the road ahead of me. I cannot know for certain where it will end. Nor do I really know myself, and the fact that I think I am following your will does not mean that I am actually doing so. But I believe that the desire to please you does in fact please you. And I hope I have that desire in all that I am doing. I hope that I will never do anything apart from that desire. And I know that if I do this, you will lead me by the right road though I may know nothing about it. Therefore, I will trust you always though I may seem to be lost and in the shadow of death. I will not fear, for you are ever with me, and you will never leave me to face my perils alone.

Thomas Merton
(1915–1968)

REFLECTION

This prayer is a moving mixture of human uncertainty blended with such deep spiritual humility and trust that it ends on a confident note of godly certainty.

The tone of the opening sentences is so uncertain that it would be possible to make the mistake of writing off the author as a no-hoper. For here is a traveller who doesn't know where he is going, can't see the road he is on and isn't sure where it will end. In his Christian life he isn't sure whether he is following God's will. A lost sheep we might think but these first impressions are deceptive.

In fact the author of this prayer was Thomas Merton, a giant of 20th-century spirituality whose books, particularly his autobiography, *The Seven Storey Mountain*, have inspired millions. An American Trappist monk who wrote and prayed in the contemplative tradition of Thomas à Kempis, Merton peels through layers of doubt and uncertainty at the beginning of the prayer until he hits the rock on which two pillars of his faith are built – holy desire and absolute trust. *I believe that the desire to please you does in fact please you*, is Merton's first assertion of spiritual trust. *I will never do anything except that desire*, is the second. Such sentiments are in harmony with à Kempis' advice in *The Imitation of Christ*: 'Desire ever and pray that the will of God be all and wholly done.'

In our journeys of surrender to God's will, we can sometimes feel lost but we need never feel afraid. Merton knows this for he ends his prayer on the confident note: *you will never leave me to face my perils alone*. A relationship with God is often perplexing, sometimes mysterious, but we are never abandoned by him. Merton's journey of faith, as proclaimed in this prayer and in his wider writing, is a beacon of hope to us all.

A Prayer to Grow in Faith

God, today I resonate with the desperate cry in the Gospel, 'I believe, help my unbelief.' Sometimes I think I operate my life out of more doubt than faith. And yet I want to believe... and I do believe.

I'm a complex creature. At times I can believe with my head, while my body is still locked into patterns of scepticism and doubt. Faith is not yet in my muscles, my bones, my glands.

Increase faith within me, O Lord. I'm sure that for faith to grow, you will put me in situations where I'll need resources beyond myself. I submit to this process.

Will this mean moving out on behalf of others, praying for them and trusting you to work in them? If so, then show me the who, what, when and where, and I will seek to act at your bidding. Throughout I am trusting you to take me from faith to faith – from the faith I do have to the faith that I am in the process of receiving.

Thank you for hearing my prayer.

Amen.   *Richard Foster*
                                        Prayers from the Heart

REFLECTION

Faith grows through experience, and all spiritual journeys include experiences of doubt. This is a wise prayer for it does not ask for the instant solution of overcoming doubt. Instead it asks to be taken on a long haul journey of experience *from faith to faith*.

Faith is tested in times of trial. When our lives go pear-shaped and blows rain in on us with inexplicable ferocity we are sometimes tempted to doubt God's faithfulness or even his existence. This is when we need reinforcements of trust. The third paragraph of this prayer recognises this when it says to God: *I'm sure that for faith to grow you will put me in situations where I'll need resources beyond myself.* These words resonate with me, for I know that I grew in faith during my prison sentence and associated dramas. This growth occurred because God blessed me with spiritual resources far greater than anything my own head or heart could possibly have provided.

If at a time of doubt I ever needed a tangible reminder of the effectiveness of praying in faith I would bring out the prayer diary I have kept for the past seven years. Its pages are full of wonderful examples of how God grows faith just as this prayer asks in its final paragraph – through experience.

The first wonder comes from looking back through the diary and seeing how many of my prayers were answered in the way requested. The second wonder is to find how many of these prayers were answered, but in different ways and in a different time scale to what was requested. The third wonder is to be reminded how I and others learned to surrender to God's will even when the prayers were not answered. The fourth wonder is to realise that the totality of these prayer experiences has somehow blended together into the gift of a far stronger faith.

Martin Luther's Prayer on Emptiness and Weakness of Faith

Behold, Lord, an empty vessel that needs to be filled. My Lord, fill it.

I am weak in the faith; strengthen thou me.

I am cold in love; warm me and make me fervent that my love may go out to my neighbour.

I do not have a strong and firm faith; at times I doubt and am unable to trust thee altogether. O Lord, help me. Strengthen my faith and trust in thee

In thee I have sealed the treasures of all I have.

I am poor; thou art rich and didst come to be merciful to the poor.

I am a sinner; thou art upright. With me there is an abundance of sin;

in thee is the fullness of righteousness.

Therefore, I will remain with thee of whom I can receive but to whom I may not give.

Amen.

Martin Luther
(1483–1546)

REFLECTION

Even the strongest believers have their moments of doubt. Such moments, which sometimes turn into longer periods, can be part of God's mysterious purposes to test us and strengthen our faith.

It may come as a surprise to learn that Martin Luther suffered from weakness of faith, emptiness of purpose and coldness of heart. Outwardly the world regarded the father of the Protestant Reformation as a leader of great certainty, conviction and courage. His fight against the sale of indulgences and his challenge to the authority of the Pope were turning points in the history of Europe and the history of Christianity. Yet inwardly Luther could at times be a fearful, doubtful, self-agonising soul.

This prayer was evidently written at one of these times. Luther is nothing if not honest before God when he says *I do not have a strong and firm faith; at times I doubt and am unable to trust thee altogether*. Yet when looked at closely the prayer can be compared to the pleas of a traveller across the sea of faith who yearns for his seasickness to end and for his strength to return. It is not a prayer of someone about to abandon ship, hence the line: *Therefore I will remain with thee.*

Remaining with Christ for the duration of the voyage requires an advanced soul to share in Christ's sufferings. This belief of Luther's is set out in his writings on the theology of the Cross. While at Wycliffe Hall, Oxford, I wrote a thesis on this complex subject which is too deep to tackle in a short reflection. However, the essence of it is reflected in the agony of this prayer. Our pain, our doubts, our poverty and our sin give us a glimpse of what Luther called the backside or dark side of the cross. It is only when we have been there that we can understand the other side of the cross in its true glory, and draw strength from it.

A Prayer to Stay Connected With God

I have just hung up; why did he telephone?
I don't know ... Oh! I get it ...
I talked a lot and listened very little.
Forgive me, Lord, it was a monologue and not a dialogue.
I explained my idea and did not get his;
Since I didn't listen, I learned nothing,
Since I didn't listen, I didn't help,
Since I didn't listen, we didn't communicate.
Forgive me, Lord, for we were connected,
And now we are cut off.

Michel Quoist
(born 1918)

REFLECTION

Getting disconnected from God is a familiar problem. But since he never hangs up on anyone and since his celestial telephone lines, unlike those of BT, AT&T, etc., are fault-free, the problem must be at our end.

Abbé Michel Quoist, a former parish priest in Le Havre composed this prayer for his thoughtful collection, *Prayers of Life*. The book opens with a meditation entitled, 'If we Knew How to Listen to God'. Its theme, well illustrated by this prayer, is that God constantly speaks to us in his Gospel and through life but, because our lives are too self-centred, we cut ourselves off from his message.

A conversation with God, which at our end consisted of a *monologue* not a *dialogue*, would be unsatisfactory for both parties. God loves to hear our needs but as part of a deeper relationship with him. Imagine how impossible it would be to build a relationship with a caller who never listened and did all the talking, usually about his or her own wish list. On the telephone or in prayer that would make a bad connection.

Jesus gave his disciples some guidance on how to stay connected to God in prayer when he told them to make their requests 'in my name'. This phrase appears four times in two short passages from St John's Gospel (John 12:13–64 and 16:23–24). The message from these verses is that we should pray in Jesus' name, i.e. in the spirit of God's will and purpose. We can only discern these when we listen to him and commit ourselves to a relationship with him.

Without such a commitment we will not understand God's calls and we will become disconnected from him. However, he will call again.

A Prayer for Self Control

O God,
Control my tongue.
Keep me from saying things which make trouble
and from involving myself in arguments
which only make bad situations worse
and which get nowhere. Control my thoughts.
Shut the door of my mind
against all envious and jealous thoughts;
shut it against all bitter and resentful thoughts;
shut it against all ugly and unclean thoughts.
Help me to live today in purity, in humility and in love.
Through Jesus Christ my Lord.

Amen.

William Barclay
(1899–1978)

REFLECTION

Self-control is a vital Christian virtue yet we all experience moments in our lives when we have difficulty in practising it. This prayer is a frank and honest appeal to God for better control of our thoughts and tongues.

One of the most quoted passages in the Bible is Galatians 5:22–23, which sets out a list of the fruit of the Spirit. Many believers know that the list begins with 'love, joy, peace'. Fewer remember that it ends with 'self control'. Christians of the early Church put great emphasis on this discipline. 'Make every effort to add to your faith, goodness; and to goodness, knowledge; and to knowledge, self control,' wrote St Peter (2 Peter 1:5–6), while St Paul reminded Timothy that God gives us 'a spirit of power, of love, and of self control' (2 Timothy 1:7).

Exercising this control needs God's help. The author of this prayer, Professor William Barclay whose Bible commentaries are read by millions, evidently had problems with his tongue and his thoughts. So do most of us. It was said of Oscar Wilde: 'He would murder his grandmother for a witty saying.' Without going that far, the temptation to make an amusing, bitchy, trouble-stirring comment can prove irresistible, as St James sternly warned: 'No man can tame the tongue. It is a restless evil full of deadly poison' (James 3:8).

If unchristian remarks are sometimes beyond our self-control, how much harder it is to avoid unchristian thoughts. The devil loves to plant them in us. Barclay's heartfelt plea, *shut the door of my mind* against bad thoughts, is a request to God we can all repeat. For the struggle between good and evil runs through every human heart. This prayer is a formidable weapon in that struggle, reinforced by its last line, *help me to live today in purity, in humility and in love.*

Shut Out Everything Except God

Come now, little man,
Turn aside for a while from your daily employment,
Escape for a moment from the tumult of your thoughts
Put aside your weighty cares,
Let your burdensome distractions wait,
Free yourself awhile for God
And rest awhile in him.
Enter the inner chamber of your soul
Shut out everything except God
And that which can help you in seeking him
And when you have shut the door, seek him.

St Anselm
(1033–1109)

REFLECTION

This is a pre-prayer meditation in which the author, St Anselm, tries to enter the right mood to pray. *Come now little man*, he says to himself, meaning in effect 'Brace up Anselm!' or perhaps more appropriately, 'Slow down Anselm!' For the essence of his message is that before we pray we should *shut out everything except God* – and then seek him.

Many of us find Anselm's advice hard to follow. It is difficult to shut the door on the intrusive pressures of 21st-century life, such as emails, traffic jams, mobile phones, commuter journeys and hectic schedules. Yet before we use these as excuses we should remember that every age has its pressures and that distraction has always been a tool of the devil.

Even Jesus had to discipline himself to escape from the distractions that surrounded him. The first account of Jesus in prayer says, 'Early in the morning while it was still dark, Jesus got up, left the house and went to a solitary place where he prayed' (Mark 1:35–37).

That description tells us something about our Lord's need for solitude and stillness in prayer. Rising before dawn and finding a lonely place were his pre-prayer disciplines. If we want to follow Jesus we should imitate these disciplines at least to the extent of shutting the door on our busy lives to have a few minutes of quiet time alone with him each day.

When we have managed to shut out everything except God, the next stage of the seeker's journey is beautifully described by the Prophet Jeremiah: 'Then you will call upon me and come and pray to me and I will listen to you. You will seek me and find me when you seek me with all your heart' (Jeremiah 29:12–13).

To Care Only for God's Approval

O Lord God, grant us always, whatever the world may say, to be content with what you say. May we care only for your approval. For the sake of Jesus Christ our Lord.

Amen.   *General Charles Gordon*
                                                    (1833–1885)

REFLECTION

This is a single-minded prayer. Its clarity and brevity are typical of its author who became a great hero of the British Empire.

Charles Gordon gave his life to Christ when he was a 21-year-old second lieutenant, recently commissioned into the Royal Engineers. A religious brother officer of evangelical views converted Gordon to the faith that dominated the rest of his life.

Although he achieved military fame and honours for his campaigns in China and Africa, General Gordon was a humble man whose passion away from the battlefield was the religious education of schoolboys. In his letters to them he wrote many prayers, mostly short and to the point.

The message of this one is: don't bother about the opinions of the world. Concentrate on winning the approval of Jesus. Keep your mind on God, not on people.

Gordon lived up to his prayer and died honouring its precepts. In 1885 when he was Governor General of the Sudan, Gordon's palace in Khartoum was besieged by a mob of extremists led by a religious fanatic known as the Mahdi. A relief expedition sent from Britain failed to arrive in time to end the siege. Twenty-four hours before the British troops reached Khartoum Gordon was assassinated by the mob on the staircase of the palace. The night before his death he wrote to his sister: 'We are on our last legs but I am quite happy, thank God, for I have tried to do my duty to him'.

After his death Gordon was venerated as a hero. By public subscription the Gordon Memorial School for Boys was founded to perpetuate his work in religious education. This prayer was regularly said at services in the school. Its words and Gordon's example are a reminder that the only approval in our lives that matters is the approval of God.

A Prayer for Perseverance

O Lord when thou givest to thy servants to endeavour any great matter, grant us also to know that it is not the beginning, but the continuing of the same unto the end until it be throughly finished which yieldeth the true glory. Through him, who for the finishing of thy work laid down his life, our Lord and Saviour Jesus Christ.

Amen.   *Sir Francis Drake*
                                                                    (1540–1596)

REFLECTION

Perseverance is an important ingredient of success in business, sport, politics and many other walks of life. The author of this prayer, the favourite admiral of Queen Elizabeth I, Sir Francis Drake, needed perseverance when he was under pressure to accomplish some of his remarkable naval exploits. He could easily have been a role model for the message proclaimed in a myriad of self-help books: If you persevere at the business in hand you will gain great rewards.

Spiritual perseverance is different. It is often seen as a testing experience involving suffering. Its rewards are spiritual gifts. The greatest of these are a stronger faith and a deeper relationship with God. Two authors of New Testament epistles highlight these virtues. 'The testing of your faith develops perseverance,' writes James. 'Perseverance must finish its work so that you may be mature and complete' (James 1:4–5). Paul goes further: 'We rejoice in our sufferings because we know that suffering produces perseverance; perseverance character, and character hope' (Romans 5:3–4).

When I say this prayer I sometimes wonder whether Sir Francis Drake wrote it because he needed perseverance for some worldly purpose on his agenda such as circumnavigating the globe. Or was he seeking the Pauline or Jamesian rewards from perseverance such as character, hope and spiritual maturity? Perhaps Drake wanted both. This would not be an impossible prayer request if the earthly goal were in accordance with God's will.

The greatness in this prayer lies in its finale: *Through him, who through the finishing of thy work laid down his life.* This reminds us that Jesus' last word from the cross was 'It is finished'. As the New Testament Greek word here, *tetelestai*, makes clear, this carries the deeper theological meaning of 'it is fulfilled' or 'it is completed'. A cry of triumph rather than a groan of relief. It was surely that sense of completeness for which Drake was praying – with perseverance.

Augustine's Prayer for Purity of Heart

Almighty God, in whom we live and move and have our being, you have made us for yourself so our hearts are restless until they rest in you. Grant us purity of heart and strength of purpose, that no selfish passion may hinder us from knowing your will or no weakness in doing it; but that in your light we may see light and in your service find perfect freedom, through Jesus Christ our Lord.

Amen.   *Augustine of Hippo*
(AD 354–430)

REFLECTION

This great prayer of Augustine of Hippo is so profound that every phrase in it can act as a wake-up call summoning us to God's service.

The only part of the prayer that is not Augustine's is the opening line defining God as the one *in whom we live and move and have our being*. This comes from St Paul's speech in Acts 17:28 to the men of Athens, and it seized their attention just as much as it still holds ours two thousand years later.

You have made us for yourself continues Augustine, reminding us that it is by God and for God's purpose that we are, in the words of the psalmist, 'fearfully and wonderfully made' (Psalm 139:7). As a consequence of our creation *our hearts are restless until they rest in you*. So many spiritual writers have tried to explain that inexplicable longing for God's presence in our lives, which we sometimes spend years trying to deny or avoid. This was the experience of Francis Thompson who wrote an anguished poem, *The Hound of Heaven*, on this theme. It was also the experience of Augustine himself who lamented his libertine years of restlessness and pointlessness without God: 'Too late have I loved you O Beauty so old and yet so new,' he wrote in his *Confessions*. 'Too late I came to love you, yet you were within me.'

Augustine understood the divine forces calling him to end his restlessness. They were *purity of heart and strength of purpose*. He also understood the satanic forces obstructing his knowledge and obedience to God's will. They were *selfish passion and weakness*. The battle between God's call and Satan's temptations are the spiritual warfare within all of us as we struggle to build our true relationship with God.

Three Crucial Questions

What have I done for Christ?
What am I doing for Christ?
What ought I to do for Christ?

St Ignatius of Loyola
(1491–1556)
Spiritual Exercises
Paragraph 53

REFLECTION

These three crucial questions come early in the *Spiritual Exercises* of St Ignatius Loyola. At the mystical conclusion to the first colloquy the exercisor is asked to gaze at the figure of Christ hanging on the cross, and then to ask them of himself or herself. For many practitioners of Ignatian spirituality this deep moment of self-interrogation is a profound supernatural experience.

Under the guidance of Father Gerard Hughes SJ, I went on a silent, nine-day Ignatian retreat on the *Spiritual Exercises* in 1998. 'Shattering' was the adjective I used in my diary to describe the most important discoveries of that retreat, especially those that flowed from these questions.

It is clear from the context of the three choices that they are not just about whether we will or will not try to live life obeying God's commandments. These questions take us far deeper towards the life of a disciple with all the discipline, suffering and sacrifice that this requires.

The challenge of the Ignatian questions bear comparison with Jesus' challenge to the rich young man in Mark 10:17–24. Here was a good and devout young man who had kept the commandments since his boyhood. But was he ready to make the sacrifice Jesus asked of him – in his case to give up his wealth? The answer was no, so the young man went away 'exceedingly sorrowful'.

There are different levels of spirituality. Perhaps the deepest is the holiness that comes from following Christ all the way to Calvary. Thomas à Kempis spelt out this spiritual challenge with brutal directness: 'Jesus has many lovers of his Kingdom but few bearers of his cross. Many desire his consolation, few his tribulation. All wish to rejoice with him, few to suffer with him. Many will follow Jesus to the breaking of the bread, few to the drinking of the cup of his Passion.'

So what the three Ignatian questions are really asking is: Are *you* among the few willing to suffer with Christ?

A Prayer for God's Mercy, Peace and Grace

Take Lord and receive, all my memory, all my will, all my understanding – everything I have and possess. For you gave these gifts to me and to you I gladly return them. Only dear Lord, in your mercy, grant me your peace and your grace, for these are enough for me.

Amen. *St Ignatius of Loyola (1491–1556)*

REFLECTION

After the Lord's Prayer, this is my favourite prayer. It was written by St Ignatius of Loyola, founder of the Society of Jesus. For me its three sentences capture the essence of a right relationship with God.

The arresting opening phrase, *take Lord and receive*, summarises the total willingness of a believing soul to surrender everything to God. The list is capable of expansion far beyond the three categories of *memory*, *will* and *understanding*. Sometimes it is a good idea to insert the specific things you would have particular difficulty giving up, such as all my money, all my good health, etc., before reaching the punch line of the first sentence – *everything I have and possess*.

The second sentence underlines the joy we should feel in giving back to God our creator all the gifts he bestowed on us in the first place. The word *gladly* can be said with an uplifted heart and voice.

The last sentence is our humble petition to Almighty God mercifully to grant us his two greatest blessings – his peace and his grace. We don't deserve and we can't earn either of them. But our willingness to surrender everything else in our lives for God's service and glory may just position us so that we are able to take and receive these amazing gifts.

PART VI
How Not to Pray

1. How Not to Pray

How Not to Pray

Let me take this other glove off
As the vox humana swells,
And the beauteous fields of Eden
Bask beneath the Abbey bells.
Here, where England's statesmen lie,
Listen to a lady's cry

Gracious Lord, oh bomb the Germans.
Spare their women for thy Sake,
And if that is not too easy
We will pardon thy Mistake.
But, gracious Lord, whate'er shall be,
Don't let anyone bomb me.

Keep our Empire undismembered
Guide our Forces by thy Hand,
Gallant blacks from far Jamaica,
Honduras and Togoland;
Protect them Lord in all their fights,
And, even more, protect the whites.

Think of what our Nation stands for,
Books from Boots' and country lanes,
Free speech, free passes, class distinction,
Democracy and proper drains.
Lord, put beneath thy special care
One-eighty-nine Cadogan Square.

REFLECTION

This is a parody not a prayer. Betjeman humour at its best. Yet when the chuckling stops there is a lot to be gleaned from this poem about how not to pray.

The 1940's lady who liked to pop into Westminster Abbey for Evensong, *Whensoever I have the time*, was out of tune with God for many reasons.

First she thought she was someone rather important. Like the Pharisee in the story of the Pharisee and the Publican (Luke 18:9–14) she addressed God with external arrogance instead of internal humility.

Secondly, she thought her sins (several of them self-evident from the parodying lines about blacks, class distinction, bombing the Germans and sending white feathers) didn't really matter. But before we laugh at her, think how many people secretly echo the couplet, *Although dear Lord I am a sinner, I have done no major crime*, as a way of justifying their semi-sinful, semi-respectable lifestyles.

An eminent Victorian bishop, Handley Moule, preaching on Romans 3:23, 'For all have sinned and fall short of the glory of God', attacked such self-justifying attitudes in these dramatic words to his congregation: 'The harlot, the murderer, the liar are short of it (i.e. God's glory) but so are you! Perhaps they stand at the bottom of the mine and you on the crest of an alp; but you are as little able to touch the stars as they are.'

The lady in Westminster Abbey probably felt secure in her comfort zone, close to the stars and to God's glory as she enjoyed the swelling *vox humana* and the pealing bells. Worship in its many forms can sometimes obscure as well as illuminate spiritual reality.

Although dear Lord I am a sinner,
I have done no major crime,
Now I'll come to Evening Service
Whensoever I have the time.
So, Lord, reserve for me a crown,
And do not let my shares go down.

I will labour for thy Kingdom,
Help our lads to win the war,
Send white feathers to the cowards
Join the Women's Army Corps,
Then wash the steps around thy throne
In the Eternal Safety zone.

Now I feel a little better,
What a treat to hear thy Word,
Where the bones of leading statesmen,
Have so often been interr'd.
And now, dear Lord, I cannot wait
Because I have a luncheon date.

John Betjeman (1906–1984)
Collected Poems

So encouraged by her majestic surroundings the lady prayed with a self-centred condescension which Betjeman meant to be ludicrous, yet which is not all that far removed from the selfish prayers many of us say from time to time.

Lord put beneath thy special care, One-eighty-nine Cadogan Square and Lord ... do not let my shares go down are, with variations, well-known, if misguided, prayer requests. Why are they wrong in the eyes of a God who encouraged us to 'Ask and it will be given you ... for everyone who asks receives' (Matthew 7:7–8)?

God likes to hear our requests but they will only be answered if they are asked in his name, i.e. in accordance with his will. Jesus made this clear in John 14:13 ('Whatever you ask in my name I will do it') and in John 15:7–8 ('If you abide in me and my words abide in you, ask whatever you will and it shall be done for you').

The lady's shopping list of selfish prejudices, presumptions and peremptory demands showed that she was a long way from abiding in the Lord or having any understanding of his will. She was asking in her name, not his. So her prayers seem unlikely to have found favour with God.

Betjeman's final couplet: *And now dear Lord I cannot wait, Because I have a luncheon date*, provides yet another message on how not to pray. It is: don't short change God. He deserves our time and our concentrated attention. He also deserves our humility, our confessions of sinfulness and the surrender of our wills to his will. All these are the opposite of what the lady in Westminster Abbey offered him. This is why, for all the amusement we derive from John Betjeman's parody, she gives us such an object lesson in how not to pray.

PART VII

Supplication

1. A Prayer for a Sense of Humour
2. A 17th-Century Nun's Prayer
3. A Prayer for Listening
4. The Prayer of Jabez
5. A Prayer to Avoid Bad Temper
6. Two Prayers about Fear
7. Two Prayers Before Taking Exams
8. A Prayer About Fear of Flying
9. A Prayer for Going through Divorce
10. A Prayer for Dealing with Enemies
11. A Parent's Prayer for a Teenager suffering
    from an Eating Disorder
12. A Prayer for Sleep
13. A Prayer for Life and Work
14. Prayers for Work
15. A Prayer for the Sighing of the Prisoner
16. Charles Colson's Prayer for those in Prison
17. A Prayer for Prisoners of Conscience
18. A Prayer for All Prisoners
19. A Prayer for Victims of Crime
20. Help me to Pray ... Restore me to Liberty
21. The Prayer for Parliament
22. A Prayer for the United States Senate
23. In Times of Pain
24. A Prayer for those who Wake or Watch or
    Weep Tonight
25. Finding God When Close to Death
26. When the Fever of Life is Over
27. A Prayer in Time of Sudden Bereavement
28. Five Prayers for those that Mourn
29. John Donne's Vision of Heaven

A Prayer for a Sense of Humour

Lord, give us a sense of humour and also things to laugh about. Give us the grace to take a joke against ourselves and to see the funny side of the things we do. Save us from annoyance, bad temper, resentfulness against our friends. Help us to laugh even in the face of trouble. Fill our minds with the love of Jesus, for his name's sake.

Amen.   *A. G. Bullivant*

REFLECTION

Without laughter and joy, life would be impossible. These two essentials of our spiritual as well as our practical journey are gifts from God. So we need to pray for them and thank him for them.

This prayer is full of wisdom as well as humour. It nudges us towards having *the grace to take a joke against ourselves*. It takes a pot shot against our self-erected barriers to laughter: *annoyance, bad temper, resentfulness*. I particularly like the request, *Help us to laugh even in the face of trouble*. This was something I learned to do during my time in prison, where I was often amused by the teasings and joshings of fellow inmates with a flair for gallows' humour.

A family example of humour in adversity was given recently by my brother-in-law, Morgan Rees-Williams. He is not exactly the most faithful of believers. Nevertheless, out of fraternal loyalty he turned up at his local church, Christ Church, Fulham, on an evangelical outreach evening when I was the main speaker.

The following morning Morgan suffered a massive heart attack. Elizabeth and I rushed round to the A&E wing at the Chelsea and Westminster hospital where we found him in intensive care. He was wired up to every imaginable cardiac care device and drip. As soon as he saw me, Morgan lifted up his oxygen mask and said: 'Good talk last night – but look where it got me.'

Jesus had a sense of humour. It comes through in the gentle irony of many of his parables and stories. He probably made his listeners laugh with inflexions of voice and tone as he told them. But the humour of Jesus was suffused with his love and compassion for humanity. So this prayer, which is all about enjoying the funny side of life, ends most appropriately and seriously: *Fill our minds with the love of Jesus*.

A 17th-Century Nun's Prayer

Lord, thou knowest better than I know myself that I am growing older and will someday be old. Keep me from the fatal habit of thinking I must say something on every subject and on every occasion. Release me from craving to straighten out everybody's affairs. Make me thoughtful but not moody; helpful but not bossy. With my vast store of wisdom, it seems a pity not to use it all, but thou knowest Lord that I want a few friends at the end.

Keep my mind free from the recital of endless details; give me wings to get to the point. Seal my lips on my aches and pains. They are increasing and love of rehearsing them is becoming sweeter as the years go by. I dare not ask for grace enough to enjoy the tales of others' pains, but help me to endure them with patience.

I dare not ask for improved memory, but for a growing humility and a lessening cocksureness when my memory seems to clash with the memories of others. Teach me the glorious lesson that occasionally I may be mistaken.

Keep me reasonably sweet; I do not want to be a Saint – some of them are so hard to live with – but a sour old person is one of the crowning works of the devil. Give me the ability to see good things in unexpected places and talents in unexpected people. And, give me, O Lord, the grace to tell them so.

Amen.

REFLECTION

We will all grow old one day. This is a prayer that we may do so with grace and humour. I would have enjoyed knowing the anonymous 17th-century nun who wrote this prayer. She was evidently a lady of sound common sense lightened by delightful touches of self-deprecating wit. You can almost hear the chuckle in her voice as she delivers lines like: *With my vast store of wisdom it seems a pity not to use it all but thou knowest Lord that I want a few friends at the end.*

The nun's requests to God are sharp and sensible. *Make me thoughtful but not moody, helpful but not bossy* is Polonius without the pomposity. Asking for *a growing humility and a lessening cocksureness* is a prayer need at any age. So is this gem for the garrulous: *Give me wings to get to the point.*

When I read this prayer I smile and think lovingly of the Irish nun who nursed me through three years of TB in Dublin's Cappagh hospital during the 1940s. Her name was Sister Mary Finbar. I cherish her memory not only because she was such a wonderful nurse, teacher and bedside companion, but also because she had about her an aura of holiness leavened with humour. This is a rare combination. My 20th-century Irish nun and this 17th-century unknown nun both had these qualities in abundance. They shine gloriously through the words of this prayer.

A Prayer for Listening

O Lord Jesus give us hearts that listen. Hearts that listen to you in silence and love. Hearts that listen to those we meet, to those in trouble, in the silence of your true compassion and understanding. Help us to remember that there is a time for silence and a time for speaking. Give us the wisdom to know when to speak and when to hold our peace. Through Jesus Christ Our Lord.

Amen.

Lady Elizabeth Basset
(1908–2000)

REFLECTION

Listening is becoming a lost art. In our hectic, noisy, often aggressive culture we need to lower our voices and make time for silence so that we may hear the whispers of God.

This prayer was written by one of the best listeners I ever met. Lady Elizabeth Basset was a contemplative Christian who collected together a beautiful anthology, *Love is My Meaning*. I was taken to meet her by a close friend, Nadine Bonsor, when my legal and media dramas were at their worst. On our afternoon visits to Lady Elizabeth she would read prayers, poems and meditations which she had prepared for the occasion. But what I remember most vividly were her long silences after each reading.

On one visit she read out this extract from *Something Beautiful for God* by Malcolm Muggeridge. 'The more we receive in silent prayer the more we can give in our active life. We need silence in order to be able to touch souls. The essential thing is not what we say, but what God says to us.'

Lady Elizabeth's prayer is not only about listening in silence to God. It also asks that we may be given hearts that can listen to other people, particularly people in trouble. This is a great spiritual gift.

'Be still and know that I am God' (Psalm 46:10) is a divine command to listen to him in silence. Most of us obey it too little. Even in our quiet times there is a tendency to get the balance wrong between listening and talking to God. So perhaps the best line of this prayer is the last: *give us wisdom to know when to speak and when to hold our peace.*

The Prayer of Jabez

And Jabez called on the God of Israel saying: 'Oh that you would bless me indeed, and enlarge my territory, that your hand would be with me and that you would keep me from evil so that I may not cause pain!'

So God granted him what he requested.

1 Chronicles 4:10
New King James Bible

REFLECTION

This Old Testament prayer has been rescued from obscurity in recent years by a small and highly successful book on it, *The Prayer of Jabez*, by Bruce Wilkinson. It spent many weeks in the number one slot on the New York Times best-seller list and has so far sold over six million copies. What is so special about it?

The key requests in the prayer each send out their own signals. *Bless me indeed* is, in the original Hebrew, a far more urgent and personal imperative than the generalised requests for a blessing on food or the ritual intonations at the end of a church service. Bruce Wilkinson is right to point out the radical aspect of Jabez's request for this blessing: 'He left it entirely up to God to decide what the blessings would be and where, when or how Jabez would receive them.'

The same *leave it to God* approach applies to the next two requests: *and enlarge my territory that your hand would be with me*. These are spiritual supplications. Jabez was not asking for his farm or bank balance to be enlarged. What he wanted was to do more for God, with God.

The final request, *Keep me from evil so that I may not cause pain*, was made because Jabez knew his sins inflicted pain. So a thousand years before Jesus taught his disciples to pray the Lord's Prayer with its phrase 'Deliver us from evil', Jabez had tuned in to the same wavelength.

The Prayer of Jabez must have pleased God. He loves to grant our requests made by prayerful hearts in accordance with his will. So the last line in this verse from 1 Chronicles says it all: *So God granted him what he requested.*

A Prayer to Avoid Bad Temper

Oh Lord, help me to stop losing my temper. Even in situations of pressure and provocation this is a failure of self-control. But I lose control as an indulgence of my frustrations or sometimes to assert my self-importance, and these are sins.

Lord, you never lost your temper for self-centred reasons even though you were sometimes angry on behalf of God your Father. So guide me away from the wrong kind of anger. Guide me away also from the self-imposed pressures that can lead to frustrated anger such as overworking, cramming too much into my schedule, becoming impatient or getting aggressive about other people's shortcomings which are no worse than mine.

Lord, have mercy upon me and forgive me such sins. Grant me the discipline and the humility to turn away from them, to apologise if I commit them, and to change my behaviour into a life that is pleasing to you. Through him who was never impatient, never ill tempered, and whose life was the perfect example of goodness, patience and loving kindness in God's service: Our Lord and Saviour Jesus Christ.

Amen.   *J.A.*

REFLECTION

Bad temper is unattractive to our contemporaries and displeasing to God. So why is there so much of it about, even among people who claim to be spiritual? The root of the problem is a lack of inner peace.

The pressures of our 21st-century world drive out inner peace and bring in outbursts of anger. Roadrage, impatience with the internet, aggression in the office and frustration with public services are just four of the daily experiences that can provoke bad temper in our modern lives, not to mention the more personal flashpoints in our individual relationships.

This prayer reminds us Jesus never lost his temper. He did occasionally get angry with the hypocrites, with those who mocked God and with the moneychangers in the temple who commercialised him. But that is a quite different kind of justified anger. In our age we might be justified in getting angry about racial discrimination, injustice or wickedness in any form.

This prayer is about self-centred and unjustified anger. Some of us need to battle against bad temper more than others. In that battle we need to lower our voices, submit to God's will, and strive to imitate Christ. 'That way,' wrote Thomas à Kempis, the author of *The Imitation of Christ*, 'we may enter the coasts of peace and quietness.'

Two Prayers about Fear

[1]

Lord, I am afraid, so I ask for your help in fighting my fear. Sometimes I don't quite know what I am afraid of. Fear of uncertainty, fear of failure, fear of being left on my own, fear of emptiness, fear of the unknown – these are the insecurities that attack me, particularly at night.

At other times my fears are specific. They are anxieties about health, money, love, loneliness and relationships. One or other of them always seems to be going wrong.

Lord I know I should trust you in such moments of fear. But my anxieties seem stronger than my trust. Help me to overcome my lack of confidence. Grant me the faith to know that the only true security comes from your perfect love which casts out all fear. Through Jesus Christ our Lord.

Amen.   *J. A.*

REFLECTION

To fear is human. All of us go through periods in our lives when we are afraid no matter how stiff we keep our upper lips. The blessing of a prayerful relationship with God is that we can open those lips and confide in him about even our most irrational fears or our darkest and most disturbing ones.

Jesus' disciples were often frightened. They were scared by storms on Lake Galilee (Mark 5:35–41); by clouds on a mountain during the transfiguration (Luke 9:34); when they thought Jesus walking on water was a ghost (Matthew 10:36). At the time of Jesus' arrest they were so terrified that they deserted him and fled (Matthew 25:56).

In the walking on the water episode Jesus called out to his disciples; 'Take courage. It is I. Don't be afraid' (Matthew 14:27). It is still his response to his fearful followers today. But often, like the disciples, we need help before we can take courage.

In my own periods of fear I have found that reading certain key passages of scripture over and over again helped me to regain confidence and courage. My favourite biblical fear-killer is a mysterious passage from Isaiah. At the height of my fear-filled troubles (which included defeat, disgrace, divorce, bankruptcy and jail) my then spiritual director, Father Gerard Hughes SJ, gave it to me to read in this version:

'Do not be afraid for I have redeemed you.
I have called you by your name, you are mine.
If you pass through the sea I will be with you.
If you go through rivers they will not swallow you up.
If you pass through the fire you will not be scorched and the flames will
    not burn you ...
So do not be afraid for I am with you ...'   *(Isaiah 43:1–5)*

[2]

I would like to rise above, Lord.
Above and beyond.
I would like to purify my glance
and borrow your eyes.

I have fears which grip so tightly.
Fears of failure, fears of success.
Fears of not being loved, fears of being
    misunderstood.
I am imprisoned by my fears.

I would like to rise above, Lord.
Above and beyond.
I am worried about yesterday.
About my failure,
and whether I can be forgiven.
I am worried about tomorrow.
All the expectations and ideals.
I long to discover today.
I long to discover the place of joy
– the place of beauty
– the place of content
the place which I know is here. So close.
And yet I love my prison and I hate it.

I long for freedom.

My child, I hear your cry.
I have long been watching your closed shutters.
Why choose to be a prisoner of yourself?
You are free.
It is not I who locked the door,
It is not I who can open it
… for it is you, from the inside,
who persist in keeping it solidly barred.

Author unknown

Although these verses from Isaiah present fear as an individual problem, in fact it is a near universal one. This was brought home to me by a remarkable sermon on fear preached on 8th August 2004 at St Matthew's, Westminster, by our Vicar, Father Philip Chester. Almost as interesting as his sermon were the reactions to it. For over a glass of wine in the garden after the service no less than six friends in the congregation (all of them so outwardly confident looking!) confided that Father Philip's text and the second prayer, printed on the page opposite, which he quoted in full, had really spoken directly to their fear problem.

His text was Luke 12: 'Fear not little flock for it is your Father's good pleasure to give you the Kingdom.'

The sermon concluded:

'When today we walk up to the altar and hold out our hands to receive Jesus in the Blessed Sacrament, let us turn aside from our fears and open our lives in faith to the Kingdom of God. For that is our faith, that is our treasure and that is where our heart must be.

Where fear imprisons, faith liberates;
Where fear paralyses, faith empowers;
Where fear disheartens, faith encourages;
Where fear sickens, faith heals;
Where fear makes useless, faith makes beautiful;
Where fear puts hopelessness at the heart of life,
faith opens the windows on to a new world,
a new life that knows no end.

Fear not, little flock, for it is your Father's good pleasure to give you the Kingdom.'

Two Prayers Before Taking Exams

[1]

Heavenly Father, you know how important this exam is to me and my future. Please help me to achieve success. Guide me into displaying my knowledge so that I may get the best possible results. Grant me productive times of revision and restful nights of sleep before each day's papers. May the questions be fair and my answers to them wise, for with you, Lord, all things are possible.

Lord help me also to remember that all wisdom, knowledge and academic successes are gifts from you and that whatever happens in this exam my goal is to serve you and please you according to your will. Through Jesus Christ our Lord.

Amen.   *J.A.*

REFLECTION

Examinations create pressures. For many students they are the toughest pressures a young life has to face in its early years. So it is natural to pray for God's help and guidance at such a testing moment.

Although many passages of scripture tell us not to worry (for example Psalm 37, which begins 'Do not fret...') it is extremely difficult for a student to follow this biblical advice when exams are looming. Yet once we have asked God for his help, the ideal state of prayerfulness is to acknowledge our gratitude for the gifts he has given us and then to surrender to his will. The final sentence of this prayer tries to do this.

I wrote this prayer with special feeling because of my recent experiences with exams as a 58-year-old mature student of Oxford University. I don't think I have ever been more nervous than I was on 28th March 2001, the day when I dressed up in full *subfusc* (dark suit, white bow tie, gown and mortarboard) and entered the Examination School's building to sit Part 1 of the Bachelor of Theology exam.

The confidence of youth had deserted me. I was particularly fearful of the Old Testament paper on which I felt less than competent. The night before the exam I prayed with great fervency with a fellow Wycliffe Hall BTh candidate, Patrick Malone, whose academic nerves were as bad as mine.

Rarely have prayers received better or quicker answers! Dream questions appeared in the exam paper the next morning on the very topics we had selected for overnight revision. Both of us received much better marks than we had dared to hope for. This anecdote should explain why I believe in prayer before an important exam!

[2]

O God we start exams tomorrow. I've studied hard but I'm sure I haven't learned enough, and I cannot always remember what I've learned.

Please help me to keep calm and not to be worried, so that I'll remember what I've learned and do my best. Then if I fail I need not be ashamed. And if I pass please help me not to boast but to give my thanks to you for helping me to use the gifts which you have given. Thank you God.

Nancy Martin

This is an attractive prayer of humility, humour and total trust in God on the eve of an examination.

The author, Nancy Martin, must surely have been a nervous young schoolgirl. There is a flustered feminine touch about the self-deprecating description of her knowledge and her memory on the eve of the exam.

But then the prayer settles down into a slower rhythm of trust and surrender to God. First, she asks for calm, for an absence of worry and *to do my best*. Next there is an acceptance of God's will. Whether she succeeds or fails she will avoid all shame or boasting. Instead, she will thank God for whatever happens.

Although this is at first glance a charming prayer for the special situation facing a young examination candidate, in fact it has a far wider application and contains profound spiritual truths. What shines through this prayer is a combination of self-help and God's help, followed by an abandonment of self to God in trust and gratitude. 'Please let me do my best then let God do the rest and I truly thank him anyway,' is the message.

The Old Testament prophet Habakkuk proclaimed a similar message in his eloquent prayer of trust:

> 'Though the fig tree does not bud, and there are no grapes on the vines;
> Though the olive crop fails, and the fields produce no food;
> Though there are no sheep in the pen and no cattle in the stalls
> Yet I will rejoice in the Lord, I will be joyful in God my Saviour.
> The Sovereign Lord is my strength, he makes my feet like the feet of a deer;
> He enables me to climb up to the high places.' *(Habakkuk 3:17–19)*

From ancient agriculture to modern examinations, if we pray to trust God and to thank him for the results, whatever they are, we will not be disappointed.

A Prayer About Fear of Flying

O Lord I am fearful as I wait for my flight to take off. Calm me, protect me, and send your heavenly angels to keep watch over those I love and those with whom I am travelling. In these times of terrorism and other dangers, deliver us from evil. For it is you Lord, you Lord only, who keeps our lives in safety. So guard us under your angels' wings and bring us to the place where you are calling us to be. Through Jesus Christ our Lord.

Amen.   *J.A.*

REFLECTION

Fear of flying can be an incentive to prayer. It is amazing how many people, who are at best occasional communicators with God, will pray to him as their aircraft rolls down the runway or when it dips and tosses when passing through turbulence. A film star of my acquaintance, bouncing around in his seat on a tempestuous flight across the Atlantic, became so frightened that in loud and terrified prayer he offered all sorts of deals to God along the lines of: 'O Lord if you will save my life I'll stop swearing, stop drinking, go to Mass on Sunday, etc., etc.'

Such panic-stricken pleas to God are irrational. Yet they are also a reminder of our instinctive desire to pray even if the instincts are only unleashed in moments of fear. Looked at rationally, modern air travel is now so safe that pedestrians crossing streets are more at risk than airline passengers crossing continents. But God often whispers to us in life's storms even though he knows we will come through them. Are we willing to listen to his whispers?

Prayers for protection are as old as time. This one may look modern with its references to air travel and terrorism but its thoughts and phrases are drawn from psalms written three thousand years ago. The two main sources of inspiration here are Psalm 91, a wonderful prayer for protection, and Psalm 4, whose key verse forms part of S. S. Wesley's famous anthem, *Lead Me Lord*: 'For it is you Lord, you Lord only, that makest me dwell in safety.'

The link between these ancient psalms and our contemporary fears of air travel is that a true and trusting relationship with God is our only security. The psalmists had such a relationship. Do you?

A Prayer for Going through Divorce

O Lord Jesus Christ we pray for your compassion for all who suffer pain from the misery of divorce, especially for the children of the marriage.

If it is your will, even at this late stage, make it possible for the fires of matrimonial love to be rekindled and for the damage to the marriage to be repaired.

But if the divorce has become inevitable, then Lord in your mercy grant forgiveness for the sins of the past and give healing for the hopes of the future. Give wisdom to the lawyers and judges in the proceedings. May the divorcing parties be freed from all bitterness and recrimination. Guide them into new lives filled with love and support for their children. May all members of this divided family receive the blessing of your fatherly care, and may they all have a fresh start in a new life with you. Through Jesus Christ our Lord.

Amen.   *J.A.*

REFLECTION

Divorces are now commonplace in contemporary society yet few, if any, religious books contain prayers for those who suffer under the pressures of a matrimonial break-up. This is because the Church rightly regards the marriage vows as sacred. Those who break them are sinners in need of God's forgiveness.

Yet the church also teaches us that no sinner, however grievous, falls below the reach of God's grace. Moreover there can be innocent parties in a divorce, especially the children of a failed marriage. So it is likely that there will be a real need for prayer when divorce proceedings are pending.

Such proceedings are almost always painful and often acrimonious. Is there such a thing as a Christian way to behave when one is engaged in such an unchristian activity as divorce? No clear guidance is given in scripture. Yet I hope it is not wrenching verses too far out of context if I suggest that the following passage from St Paul's letter to the Philippians is a good guide to human behaviour at all times, including and perhaps especially in those times when we are under maximum pressure, such as during the break-up of a marriage:

'Finally brethren, whatsoever things are true, whatsoever things are honest, whatsoever things are just, whatsoever things are pure, whatsoever things are lovely, whatsoever things are of good report. If there be any virtue and if there be any praise, think on these things' (Philippians 4:8–9).

Reflecting on the good things that happened in a marriage which is ending may not only be a useful guide to right conduct about the old life in a divorce; it could also set some signposts for the new life in the years ahead. As St Paul says, 'Think on these things'.

A Prayer for Dealing with Enemies

Bless those who persecute you: bless and do not curse.

Do not repay anyone evil for evil. Be careful to do what is right in the eyes of everybody

If it is possible, as far as it depends on you, live at peace with everyone.

Do not take revenge my friends but leave room for God's wrath, for it is written: 'It is mine to avenge; I will repay,' says the Lord.

Do not be overcome by evil, but overcome evil with good.

Romans 12:14,17–19, 21

REFLECTION

If we are unfortunate enough to have enemies, we often deal with them badly. These five verses from St Paul's letter to the Romans are the apostle's teaching on how to deal with them well.

Each verse contains a negative exhortation followed by a positive one. So we are told not to curse but to bless (verse 14); we are not to retaliate but to do what is right and live at peace (verses 17–18); we are not to take revenge but to leave that judgement to God (verse 19); and we are not to overcome evil but to overcome evil with good (verse 21).

Following these precepts is not easy, which is why we need to pray about them. When I was in the bear-pit of politics I behaved like an angry grizzly towards the bear baiters, eventually with disastrous results to myself. I wish I had thought about the example of Jesus who never hit back in word or deed. Unfortunately non-retaliation is difficult in a culture whose softest voices say: 'Don't get mad, get even'. Strong men do both, and are often applauded for it.

Imitating Christ will bring us heavenly applause. That is a far greater goal than settling scores on earth. We should pray, in the words of this passage from Romans, for the grace to take the higher path. If you are having trouble from an enemy, before going down the low road of retaliation try reading these verses aloud two or three times and then saying this twenty-word prayer:

O Lord give me the grace to follow your example and St Paul's teaching when I respond to my enemies.

Amen.

A Parent's Prayer for a Teenager Suffering from an Eating Disorder

Heavenly Father, have mercy on N. your daughter suffering from an eating disorder. She looks so frail and wan. Her weight loss is frightening. So is the loss of her old happiness, energy and joy.

Lord, she is your daughter as well as ours. It cannot be your will that she should be suffering in this way for reasons which she does not understand, and which we, her parents, do not understand either.

So Lord, look down with loving kindness and compassion on N. Stretch out your healing hand to lift the psychological and physical blockages that have caused this disorder. Grant her a full return to good health, vitality and normal weight. And when you have restored her, lead her to live in you as a whole and happy child of God. Through Jesus Christ our Lord.

Amen.   *J.A.*

REFLECTION

Eating disorders have become a new and bewildering health problem among many young people. They take different forms but perhaps the most frequent manifestation of them occurs in the lives of teenage girls suffering from anorexia.

In our family we have had to grapple with this problem. Seeing a happy and healthy teenage granddaughter change into a gaunt and ghostly scavenger weighing less than seven stone (ninety-eight pounds) was a frightening experience which distressed the whole family and was the subject of intense prayer.

Jesus loved children and healed many of them during his earthly journey. So it is natural to pray to him for the healing of a troubled teenage child trapped in an eating disorder.

Such prayers can have many variations. Because the root of an eating disorder is more psychological than physical, the prayer needs may include understanding, patience, firmness, gentleness, mutual forgiveness and a sense of God's timing as well as the gift of God's healing, for these are deep waters.

There are two themes in this prayer that are common to all eating disorders, whatever label applies to them. The first is a reminder that all our children are God's children too.

The second theme, reflected in the final line of the prayer is that life is about spiritual wholeness as well as physical health. After Jesus said, 'Suffer the little children to come unto me,' he took the children in his hands, put his hands on them and blessed them (Mark 10:14–16). Faced with the complexity of a teenage psychological disorder to do with eating, a return to the spiritual simplicity of a child blessed by God is what we should pray for.

A Prayer for Sleep

All praise to thee, my God this night
For all the blessings of the light!
Keep me, O keep me, King of Kings,
Beneath thy own Almighty wings.

Forgive me, Lord, for thy dear Son,
The ill that I this day have done;
That with the world, myself and thee
I, ere I sleep, at peace may be.

O may my soul on thee repose,
And with sweet sleep my eyelids close –
Sleep that may me more vigorous make
To serve my God when I awake.

Thomas Ken
(1637–1711)

REFLECTION

Although better known as a hymn, these verses make a perfect ending to evening or night prayers. The first stanza begins with an expression of adoration coupled with gratitude for the day that is over. The second is a prayer of confession. The last four lines are a request for sleep – with a purpose.

Thomas Ken, who wrote this prayer, was a 17th-century clergyman of principle and courage. His parish was in Winchester, which provided him with a large vicarage. In 1668 King Charles II made a royal visit to Winchester. Looking around for a comfortable billet in which to install his courtesan, Nell Gwynne, his eye lighted on Thomas Ken's spacious residence. Could Nell lodge with you? asked His Majesty.

In those days such a royal request was virtually a royal command. But Thomas Ken said no to the King. Nell Gwynne had such a bad reputation that a God-fearing clergyman could not have her under his roof – especially as she was staying there for the purposes of royal indiscretion.

Thomas Ken's refusal could easily have got him into trouble. We may speculate that he could have had a sleepless night or two wondering what royal reprisals were coming his way. Or perhaps he just prayed this prayer, no doubt with special emphasis on the request to sleep in peace with God and the world.

Fortunately the merry monarch loved to surprise. Far from ousting Thomas Ken from his house and parish, as some observers had predicted, King Charles II made him Bishop of Bath and Wells. The reason for this preferment, explained the King, is 'I admire your courage'. It was a happy illustration of the old adage that virtue wins its own reward, which no doubt included many more nights of peaceful sleep.

A Prayer for Life and Work

God give me work
Till life shall end
And life
Till my work is done.

on the gravestone of
novelist Winifred Holtby
(1898–1935)

REFLECTION

Not everyone wants to retire. Or even if they do, their idea of retirement is not indolence or emptiness. They like the idea of taking on some other kind of work, perhaps for charity, for good causes, or for God.

In Alfred, Lord Tennyson's poem, *Ulysses*, the hero of that name says:

'How dull it is to pause, to rest a while
To rust unburnished, not to shine in use
As though to breathe were life.'

He had a point. So did Winifred Holtby, the Yorkshire novelist who wrote this prayer and asked for it to be inscribed on her gravestone. Authors and artists often go on working far beyond retirement age, perhaps because they are still full of the creative spirit or perhaps just because they have to work to pay the bills. But in any walk of life it seems appropriate to pray for work and life span to coincide.

What is work in this context? When we are past the normal age of retirement it is unusual to be still ploughing the fields or sitting in offices running businesses. But if we love God perhaps there is some work we can do in his service. It could be for 'the least of these my brethren' who are hungry, homeless, poor or in prison. It could be service to a church or to some godly good cause. But work it should be, for 'love is never lazy,' as St Augustine said.

Inevitably there will come a time when our work is done. On the eve of his crucifixion Jesus prayed to his Father: 'I have finished the work you gave me to do' (John 17:4). It may not be life's successful people who will echo our Lord's words. His servants tend to grind away obeying his purposes in weakness, in obscurity, in self-effacement and sometimes in suffering. But they too can say Winifred Holtby's prayer. They alone will be able to add to it: 'I have finished the work you gave me to do.'

Prayers for Work

A Prayer for a Job Applicant
O Lord I am a little fearful as I go out looking for a job. Please help me with my preparations as I search for the right employment. Guide me as I write my CV. Strengthen my confidence when I go to interviews. Grant me the skills to present myself well.

Lord, you who know all things will know when a job is right or wrong for me. So I pray that you will direct my footsteps into paths which are pleasing to you. Teach me wisdom and clear communication when I meet potential employers. Keep me truthful in my answers to questions. Give me patience to live with delays and resilience to cope with rejection.

At all times may my trust in you remain steadfast, knowing that you are the voice of my truest callings and the heart of my deepest hopes. Through Jesus Christ our Lord. Amen.

J. A.

A Prayer to Ease the Fear of Unemployment
O God who rejoices in both our work and our play, I come before you unemployed, afraid, shaken in my trust.

When I lose courage and hope while searching for work, be my rock of safety.

When I find it hard to believe in my talents, revive in me an appreciation of the gifts you have given me.

When I begin to doubt my worth, help me to remember that I do not need to earn your love.

When my fears take hold and start to overwhelm me, let me find comfort in your care for me and those I love, and in their love for me.

Thank you for all those who continue to support and encourage me during this difficult time. May it somehow bring us closer to one another and to you.

Kathleen Fischer and Thomas Hart

REFLECTION

These four contemporary prayers deal with a category of life's pressures, which is surprisingly neglected in most anthologies and prayer books. The category is that of work, particularly the difficult aspects of it, such as looking for a job and fear of redundancy.

There are few more stressful situations than losing a job and having to cope with the subsequent travails of unemployment. It is natural that anyone facing such pressures should want to pray about them. The same goes for anyone going through the experiences of applying for a job or going for an audition.

I see something of these experiences within our own family, for my wife, Elizabeth, and I between us have seven children of employment age. Four of them are in the notoriously uncertain world of film and theatre (hence the inclusion of a prayer for auditions and screen tests), while the other three have all had their ups and downs when it comes to earning their livings. Such uncertainties are now typical of modern employment patterns. Long-term job security used to be normal in most post-war economies. But about 30 years ago the world of work changed. Jobs for life have become almost unknown. We now live in a world of short-term contracts, instant lay-offs, frequent job applications and inevitable periods of unemployment.

The key to these four prayers is that they put God at the centre of our employment hopes and anxieties. *May it somehow bring us closer to one another and to you*, say Kathleen Fischer and Thomas Hart at the end of their anguished prayer about the fears that unemployment generates. *As I search for new and better employment may I also search for a new and deeper relationship with you O Lord*, is the final sentence of the prayer about redundancy. The prayer for auditions asks for *wisdom to understand that whatever I do on screen or stage comes from your goodness and is offered for your glory.*

A Prayer About Redundancy

O Lord the blow of redundancy has fallen painfully upon me. Have mercy on me and on my family at this difficult time. May we survive both emotionally and financially. May we be strengthened both prayerfully and spiritually. As I search for new and better employment may I also search for a new and deeper relationship with you, O Lord, the foundation of all favours and giver of all gifts, our Saviour Jesus Christ.

Amen.   *J.A.*

A Prayer for Those Going to Auditions and Screen Tests

Heavenly Father, all gifts come from you so I thank you for these career opportunities with which you have blessed me.

Like the first two servants in Jesus' parable of the talents, I long to develop my talent to the full in order to please you.

So Lord, be with me as I go for my audition (or screen test). If it is your will I pray that I may succeed in getting the part. If I do not succeed I pray that I will not feel disappointed. Above all I pray for the wisdom to understand that whatever I do on screen or stage comes from your goodness and is offered for your glory. Through Jesus Christ our Lord.

Amen.   *J.A.*

The centrality of God in our working lives is vital, particularly when things go wrong. There is an interesting psalm on this theme, Psalm 4, which is all about wealthy men falling out and making the life of one of their former colleagues (the psalmist) a complete misery. The rich bosses probably sacked him, for the psalmist begins with the cry: 'O God, give me relief from my distress.' This is the prayer of many a breadwinner when thrown out on the street. But the psalmist ends with verses that recognise that God has answered his prayer with something even more important than a secure job: 'You have filled my heart with greater joy than when their grain and new wine abound. I will lie down and sleep in peace, for you alone, O Lord, make me dwell in safety.' (Psalm 4:7–8)

For what the psalmist has discovered, is that compared to the pleasures of successful materialism in ancient Israel 'when new wine and grain abound', or of good salaries and bonuses in the 21st century market economy, the individual who has God at the centre of his or her life gains a far richer reward.

If we accept that God is our only security, everything else falls into place. Of course he listens to our prayers for employment. 'Give us this day our daily bread' was a key request in the prayer that Jesus taught us. In his Sermon on the Mount (see Matthew 6:25–34) he also taught us not to worry about the ups and downs of our economic circumstances. This is not easy when we are unemployed. But God knows our needs and will grant our requests provided we put him at the centre of our prayer life and working life.

A Prayer for the Sighing of the Prisoner

O God, let the sighing of the prisoner come before you and mercifully grant unto us that we may be delivered by your almighty power from all bonds and chains of sin whether in our bodies or in our souls. Through Jesus Christ our Lord.

Amen.   *Roman Breviary*

REFLECTION

The sighing of the prisoner is a vivid phrase that strikes a deep chord with me (for there were many such sounds during my seven months in jail) but it may also resonate to a far wider world of sighers than those incarcerated by the state.

There are different kinds of captivity. Many people in the world of freedom are prisoners because of their unhappy lifestyles, unsatisfying careers, financial anxieties, professional disappointments or personal worries. Some of these categories will include prisoners of sin, a fact that this prayer acknowledges in its reference to *all bonds and chains of sin*. How do such captives regain their freedom?

Sighing sounds a negative activity but it can be turned into a positive one if the word is transformed by the prisoner into 'praying'. If the prisoner moves away from sighs of despair, denial or self-pity and turns them into the prayers of a soul reaching out to God, then a spiritual journey has begun.

Adversity is often the gateway to a new or deeper faith. As Martin Luther said, 'It is in our pain and in our brokenness that we can come closest to Christ.' Prisoners are frequently in such depths. But they need not stay in them.

As countless sinners, including this one, have discovered, the liberation of the Holy Spirit and the freedom of a new life in Christ are promises that will be granted to those who turn to God in penitence and faith. The journey towards receiving the great blessing of this promise can begin with the *sighing of the prisoner*.

Charles Colson's Prayer for those in Prison

Lord, thank you for becoming our brother. I ask that you would free those in prison from the bondage of their sin and their shame. Let them see prison as a time to share in the sufferings of their brothers. And to know that you share in those pains as well. Through Jesus Christ our Lord.

Amen.

Charles Colson

REFLECTION

Charles Colson is the founder of Prison Fellowship (PF), a remarkable ministry that cares for prisoners and prisoners' families in 108 countries. In America alone PF brings the Gospel to over 300,000 prisoners a year; delivers 600,000 Christians' presents to the children of prisoners; and has given vacations to over 20,000 of these children in Christian summer camps.

I have often accompanied Colson into jails in recent years while writing his biography (*Colson: A Life Redeemed*, to be published by Continuum in September 2005). He is a brilliant communicator with prisoners, making the most of that invisible bond which unites inmates with ex-offenders who come back into prison with a message of faith and hope.

This prayer pulls no punches about the shame and suffering prisoners must go through, for there can be no true penitence without pain. Colson knows this well. He serviced a seven-month sentence in 1974 for Watergate-related offences committed when he was a top White House aide to President Richard Nixon. Colson found being convicted of sin far worse that being convicted by the courts. So deep was his remorse that he decided to dedicate the rest of his life to the service of Christ.

The results of that service have been the greatest good to come out of Watergate. Colson has redeemed his own life and the lives of hundreds of thousands more by his prison ministry, his books and his evangelism. It was not the life which Colson the lawyer and politician planned for himself but he has become the embodiment of Romans 8:28: 'In all things God words for the good of those who love him who have been called according to his purpose.'

A Prayer for Prisoners of Conscience

Lord Jesus, you experienced in person torture and death as a prisoner of conscience. You were beaten and flogged and sentenced to an agonising death though you had done no wrong.

Be now with prisoners of conscience throughout the world. Be with them in their fear and loneliness, in the agony of physical and mental torture, and in the face of execution and death. Stretch out your hands in power to break their chains. Be merciful to the oppressor and the torturer and place a new heart within them.

Forgive all injustice in our lives and transform us to be instruments of your peace, for by your wounds we are healed.

from The Lion Prayer Collection
attributed to Amnesty International

REFLECTION

Prison is an ordeal for those who have done wrong and been justly punished. It is an abomination for those who have done no wrong and are suffering unjust imprisonment. Around the world the largest category of such prisoners is prisoners of conscience – which often means prisoners of religious conscience.

I have met many men and women who have been imprisoned for their religious beliefs through my voluntary work for Christian Solidarity Worldwide (CSW). This is a wonderful charity, led by Baroness Cox and Mervyn Thomas, which sets out to be 'a voice for the voiceless', speaking out and campaigning for those who are being persecuted for their faith. Astonishingly, religious persecution is on the increase in the 21st century. I have seen it with my own eyes on my travels for CSW across Asia, meeting persecuted Christians who have been imprisoned in countries like Burma, North Korea, Laos and China.

Public campaigning against such persecution starts with private prayer. It is the spiritual engine with which charities like CSW arouse the conscience of the civilised world and strengthen the victims of persecution in the oppressed world.

This prayer starts with the reminder that Jesus himself was a prisoner of conscience. He knew the agony of torture and, in his case, a cruel death. 'Father forgive them for they know not what they do,' was his prayer for the soldiers nailing him to the cross. So he will surely respond to the line: *Be merciful to the oppressor and torturer*. Even more he will know the power of the plea in the final words of the prayer: *Transform us to be instruments of your peace, for by your wounds we are healed*. The cause of prisoners of conscience is a cause dear to the heart of God.

A Prayer for All Prisoners

O Lord our heavenly Father, put love into our hearts for all who are in prison. Help us to remember them with prayers of compassion. Help them to know you in prayers of contrition. Look after their loved ones especially their little ones. Show them your mercy, teach them your patience, grant them your peace. Through him who told us not to judge others and in whose sight no sinner can be justified yet all can be forgiven, our Lord and Saviour Jesus Christ.

Amen.   *J. A.*

REFLECTION

There is a shortage of prayers for prisoners, or so it seems after trawling through numerous anthologies and books of prayer. This is surprising, for scripture is strong in its commands for us to visit and pray for those who are in jail. 'Remember those in prison as if they were your fellow prisoners,' says the author of the letter to the Hebrews (Hebrews 13:3). While Jesus, in the parable of the sheep and the goats (Matthew 25:31–46) praised those who visited 'the least of these my brothers' in prison.

While serving my sentence I received over 6000 letters, most of them from complete strangers, which in one way or another said: 'I am praying for you'. I was overwhelmed by the love and compassion expressed by those correspondents whose prayers made such a difference. In the light of their letters I came to believe that I was protected from all physical and verbal aggression during my seven months in jail by a supernatural wall of prayer. I also know that my own spiritual searchings were immeasurably enriched by prayers from beyond the walls.

Most prisoners are not as well blessed. Many have no one to pray for themselves or for their families. Their number one prayer need is usually for their children. For themselves they often need penitence, patience, peace and a relationship with their Saviour. I have written this prayer with those priorities in mind.

A Prayer for Victims of Crime

O Lord, grant your compassion and your healing to victims of crime. We ask for your special mercy for those who have been physically injured or mentally traumatised. Comfort them in their ordeals; heal their wounds, soothe their pain and calm their fears. Restore their sense of safety, granting them sleep at night and security by day.

If these victims of crime have had possessions stolen, property damaged or money embezzled, we pray that by some means or other restoration will be made to them. May they one day be ready to forgive those who have trespassed against them just as you are ready to forgive all those who have trespassed against you.

Through Jesus Christ our Lord.

Amen.   *J.A.*

REFLECTION

Victims of crime need our sympathy and our prayers. Sometimes they can also benefit from a new idea that is gradually gaining ground in several countries, called Restorative Justice.

The first wrongdoer to implement the principles of Restorative Justice as a result of an encounter with Jesus was Zaccheus, a corrupt tax collector from Jericho. His life was so transformed that he publicly apologised in front of the community for his crimes. He also paid back the money he had swindled from his victims four times over. The story which is told in Luke 19:1–9 ends with Jesus going to supper with Zaccheus, and saying: 'Today salvation has come to this house.'

Those of us who work in prison ministry have a special responsibility to pray for the victims of crime and to get the prisoners with whom we pray to understand what they have done to their victims. If such prayers lead to sincere repentance it may be appropriate for apologies and restoration to victims to follow.

There are now Christian Restorative Justice prisons in America (showing re-offending rates of eight per cent!) and in other countries. Restorative Justice schemes known as The Sycamore Tree Courses (because Zaccheus came down from a sycamore tree to meet Jesus) are working well in several British prisons. For some offenders and their victims Restorative Justice is an idea whose time has come.

None of this happens easily. Victim awareness, apologies in the community, restoration, forgiveness and reconciliation, are key ingredients in Restorative Justice but they all need prayer. The praying should begin with compassion for the victims of crime.

Help me to Pray ... Restore me to Liberty

O God, early in the morning I cry to you.
Help me to pray,
and to concentrate my thoughts on you:
I cannot do this alone
In me there is darkness,
    but with you there is light;
I am lonely;
    but with you there is help;
I am restless,
    but with you there is peace.
In me there is bitterness,
    but with you there is patience;
I do not understand your ways,
    but you know the way for me...
Restore me to liberty,
And enable me so to live now
    that I may answer before you and before me.
Lord, whatever this day may bring,
your name be praised.

Dietrich Bonhoeffer
(1906–1945)

REFLECTION

This prayer was composed by Dietrich Bonhoeffer in his prison cell. He was a Lutheran pastor who wrote several books of theology, including *The Cost of Discipleship*, a poignant title considering the cost he had to pay for his own discipleship.

Bonhoeffer was one of surprisingly few German Christians who openly opposed Hitler's policy towards the Jews. Appalled by the evils of the Nazi regime, he became involved in a conspiracy to assassinate Hitler. The plot was detected at an early stage and Bonhoeffer was arrested. While in prison he wrote many powerful letters, poems and prayers. This one is an eloquent cry to God, opening with the appeal: *Help me to pray and to concentrate my thoughts on you*. It goes on to echo the pleas of many prisoners for God's help in dealing with their feelings of loneliness, feebleness, restlessness and bitterness. The request, *Restore me to liberty*, is balanced by the obedient submission to God's will: *Lord whatever the day may bring, your name be praised*.

Bonhoeffer was executed by hanging just a few days before the war ended. His last words on the way to the scaffold were:

'This is the end, but for me, it is the beginning of life.'

The certainty of Bonhoeffer's faith, the power of his writing and the tragedy of his death has made him one of the greatest Christian martyrs of the 20th century. His relationship with God in prayer, so beautifully expressed in these words, has inspired millions of believers.

The Prayer for Parliament

Almighty God, by whom alone Kings reign, and Princes decree justice; and from whom alone cometh all counsel, wisdom and understanding; We thine unworthy servants, here gathered together in thy Name, do most humbly beseech thee to send down thy heavenly wisdom from above, to direct and guide us in all our consultations; And grant that, we having thy fear always before our eyes, and laying aside all private interests, prejudices, and partial affections, the result of all our counsels may be the glory of thy blessed name, the maintenance of true religion and justice, the safety, honour, and happiness of the Queen, the public welfare, peace and tranquillity of the realm, and the uniting and knitting together of the hearts of all persons and estates within the same, in true Christian love and charity one towards another, through Jesus Christ our Lord and Saviour.

Amen.   *House of Commons' Prayer*
                                                      circa 1661

REFLECTION

This prayer is little known outside the Palace of Westminster but well known to MPs of my generation and many previous generations. It was said daily by the Speaker's Chaplain before every sitting of the House of Commons from 1661 until 1997 when it was replaced (regrettably in my view) by a shorter and more modern version.

It may be my own familiarity with this prayer, which I heard innumerable times during my 23 years in Parliament, that gives its words such profound meaning for me. Yet there are powerful messages here to any institution which governs or legislates.

The opening sentence; *Almighty God by whom alone Kings reign and Princes decree justice and from whom alone cometh all wisdom, counsel and understanding*, is a pointed theological reminder to politicians of the ultimate source of their power.

The instruction to *lay aside all private interests, prejudices and partial affections* is a useful nudge in the direction of high standards in public life.

As for *the results of all our counsels*, i.e. the ideals of Parliament, this could hardly be a better list, ending up with the marvellous mission statement, *the uniting and knitting together of the hearts of all persons and estates in true Christian love.*

In the divisive battle of party politics the sentiments of this prayer are alas more honoured in the breach than in the observance. But parliamentary government at its best can be a great uplifter and unifier, particularly in times of crisis.

Praying for the ideals and values that underpin parliamentary government is surely a worthwhile supplication. Also anyone whose vocation lies in the life of parliamentary service may find this prayer, if they live by it, a source of encouragement to their integrity and a cause of reduction on their pressure.

A Prayer for The United States Senate

Lord Jesus, as we pray for the members of this body, its officers, and all those who share in its labours, we remember that you were never in a hurry and never lost your inner peace even under pressure greater than we shall ever know.

But we are only human.

We grow tired.

We feel the strain of meeting deadlines, and we chafe under frustration.

We need poise and peace of mind, and only you can supply the deepest needs of tired bodies, jaded spirits, and frayed nerves.

So give us your peace and refresh us in our weariness, that this may be a good day with much done and done well, that we may say with your servant Paul, 'I can do all things through Christ, who gives me strength.'

Amen.

Peter Marshall
(1903–1949)

REFLECTION

This is a prayer for the United States Senate written by its 54th Chaplain, the Revd Dr Peter Marshall, and read to the assembled Senators before the opening of the day's proceedings on 12th June 1948.

Although it is a most appropriate prayer for the members of the world's most powerful legislature, it is suitable for almost any gathering of overworked, tired and pressurised people.

The prayer opens with a reminder of the example of Jesus who never was in a hurry and never lost his inner peace even when under pressure far greater than we shall ever know. It ends with St Paul's tribute to the source of all his apostolic power: 'I can do all things through Christ who gives me strength' (Philippians 4:13). In between are the Senate Chaplain's priority requests to God for his flock's frustrations, strains, tired bodies, jaded spirits and frayed nerves. It's a familiar list of pressures which will strike a chord not just on Capitol Hill but among busy people in every walk of life.

Peter Marshall was a remarkable spiritual leader with a gift for composing prayers. He started life as a steelworker in Scotland before emigrating to America in the 1920s where he became a US citizen, a theologian and the pastor of a large Presbyterian church in Washington DC. Until his appointment as Chaplain to the US Senate in 1947, that body's prayers consisted of a somewhat perfunctory 'grace' at the start of the day's business. Marshall changed that practice. He spent hours writing a prayer for each sitting of the Senate. They had to be short for there was a strict two-minute time limit on the Chaplain's devotions. This prayer is one of Marshall's best, succinctly reminding the Senators that only God can supply their deepest needs.

In Times of Pain

Lord God,
In your compassion, come close
To those who cry out in pain,
To all who are sleepless with worry,
And to any who are physically
Or mentally wounded.

Convince us that what matters is healing
Is not a magic formula,
Or a special form of prayer,
But simply the willingness to enlarge
Our trust in your presence.

May your presence encourage
Those who nurse and tend the sick
Or wait and weep
As loved ones cling to life.

Jane Grayshon
from In Times of Pain

REFLECTION

Pain can separate us from God or bring us nearer to him. Sometimes it is a close call which way the experience will take us. So those in pain need prayer, not only for the process of healing but also for the presence of the Lord in their lives at this most testing of times.

This prayer was written by a contemporary Church of England vicar's wife, Jane Grayshon, who in recent years has suffered excruciating pain from surgery, and complicated infections. She has written two remarkable books about her experiences, *In Times of Pain* and *Treasures of Darkness*. Both emphasise, as her prayer does, the importance of keeping the lines of communication open to God during an ordeal of pain. The ancient psalmists who write poems to God about their physical and mental agonies (see, for example, Psalm 6) delivered the same message.

This prayer's message is that one way of passing the test of pain is to keep trusting in the Divine presence. Another is to be strengthened by the human presence of those who wait, weep and pray alongside their loved ones. Anyone who has their moments of agonised despair during such a journey should remember the Cross. Jesus' terrible sufferings and his despairing cry, 'My God, my God why have you forsaken me,' were followed three days later by a glorious triumph.

The bridge between Jesus' human pain and his heavenly glory was the obedient bond of trust between the Son and the Father. May the same obedience and trust be our bridge out of pain and into a deeper relationship with the Lord.

A Prayer for those who Wake or Watch or Weep Tonight

Watch O Lord with those who wake or watch or weep
   tonight,
and give your saints and angels charge over those who
   sleep.
Tend your sick ones O Lord Christ.
Rest your weary ones.
Soothe your suffering ones.
Bless your dying ones.
And all for your love's sake.

Amen.   *Augustine of Hippo*
                                          (AD 354–430)

REFLECTION

This prayer, by Augustine of Hippo, is often said at services of Compline, at sickbeds and at the hour of death. After the mood-catching alliteration of the opening line, the prayer switches to six staccato sentences, which, with exquisite economy of words, cover most nocturnal anxieties. The ending, *And all for your love's sake*, is a characteristic Augustinian crescendo.

Augustine wrote more powerfully and beautifully about love than almost any other early Christian sage. 'Love – and then do what you like,' was one of his famous sayings, quoted almost as often as his 'Our hearts are restless until they rest in you.'

Here is a less well-known passage from Augustine's essay on the Trinity in which he attempts to define Christian love:

> 'What is this kind of love, spoken of so highly by divine scripture? It is the kind of love that causes us to forsake all other ways of thinking and acting as to pursue what will be the highest good, for each man and woman we meet. "Love" describes the activity of one who has determined in his heart to be a lover. His love is not in word only. It results in loving treatment of another person. So here we find the perfect circle of Godly love; the one who determines to love in spirit; the person we choose to love despite their outward appearance or actions; and the flaming force of Godly love.'

In a different piece of writing, his homily on 1 John 6, Augustine says, 'Love is the gift that brings us into greatest intimacy with God.'

That intimacy is surely strong and real in the situations described in the requests of this prayer. God will never be far from us when we bring our evenings to a close by praying for the sick, the suffering, the weary and the dying.

Finding God When Close to Death

Look, God, I have never spoken to you,
And now I want to say 'How do you do?'
You see, God, they told me you did not exist,
And I, like a fool, believed all this.
Last night, from a shell-hole, I saw your sky,
I figured that they had told me a lie.
Had I taken time before to see things you had made,
I'd sure have known they weren't calling a spade a spade.

I wonder, God, if you would shake my poor hand?
Somehow I feel you would understand.
Strange I had to come to this hellish place
Before I had time to see your face.
Well, I guess, there isn't much more to say,
But I'm glad, God, that I meet you to-day.
The zero hour will soon be here,
But I'm not afraid to know that you're near.

The signal has come – I shall soon have to go,
I like you lots – this I want you to know.
I am sure this will be a horrible fight;
Who knows: I may come to your house tonight.
Though I wasn't friendly to you before,
I wonder, God, if you'd wait at your door:
Look, I'm shedding tears – me shedding tears!
Oh! I wish I'd known you these long, long years.
Well, I have to go now, dear God. Good-bye,
But now that I've met you I'm not scared to die.

lines discovered on the dead body of an American
soldier killed in action in North Africa, 1944.
(from Uncommon Prayers, *collected by*
Cecil Hunt, Hodder and Stoughton, 1948)

REFLECTION

'Foxhole conversions' are sometimes sneered at. These lines are convincing evidence that they can be totally sincere. They were written in or near a foxhole by a US soldier in North Africa in 1944, who was killed in action soon afterwards.

God speaks to us at different moments in our lives, including those when we should be most ready to listen to him. This soldier got his first glimpse of God by gazing at the night sky. It is a common spiritual experience shared by many across the millennia. 'The heavens declare the glory of God, the skies proclaim the work of his hands ... night after night they display knowledge,' wrote the author of Psalm 19, some three thousand years before this soldier saw God revealing himself through the same skies in 1944.

The lateness of the hour when we enter into a committed relationship with God does not bother him. He showed this by the example of the penitent thief on the cross (Luke 23:39–43) and by the parable of the labourers in the vineyard (Matthew 20:1–16). This soldier was a latecomer too. But he saw where, *like a fool*, he had gone wrong in the past; he wept tears of penitence; and he knew he had experienced a real encounter with God. The strongest evidence that his conversion was real is the line, *but now that I've met you I'm not scared to die.* May we all be blessed by such a strong faith when we come near to the hour of our death.

When the Fever of Life is Over

O Lord, support us all the day long of this troublous life until the shades lengthen, the evening comes, the busy world is hushed and our work is done. Then Lord, in thy mercy, grant us a safe lodging, a holy rest and peace at the last. Through Jesus Christ our Lord.

Amen.   *John Henry Newman*
                                                        (1801–1890)

REFLECTION

This prayer, written by Cardinal Newman, is much loved and often used at funeral or memorial services. Its words have profound meanings for anyone pondering on the riches of eternity.

The first sentence of the prayer creates peaceful images of a soul's journey through the closing stages of *this troublous life* as *the shades lengthen* and *the evening comes*. However, it is the three requests in the second sentence that lead to deeper reflection.

What do we hope and pray that God will grant us after our death? Newman's phrases provide a reassuring answer to this question.

A safe lodging reminds us of Jesus' comforting words in John 14:2, translated in the King James Bible: 'Let not your heart be troubled ... In my father's house are many mansions. If it were not so I would have told you. I go to prepare a place for you.'

A holy rest in the lodging of God's house offers a picture of perfect serenity in heaven with the one who is holy.

Peace at the last takes us still further into the unknown realms of heavenly holiness. For God's peace is indescribable. Attempts to define it such as 'that peace which the world cannot give' or 'the peace of God which passeth all understanding' (both from the *Book of Common Prayer*) fall far short of what God, in his mercy, may be preparing for his faithful servants. Newman's genius was to offer in this short prayer some visionary glimpses of eternal rest.

A Prayer in Times of Sudden Bereavement

Lord, this dreadful thing has happened and our minds are baffled, our spirits weighed down with grief.

It is beyond our understanding why this life should be taken, or why we should be called upon to suffer so terrible a loss.

Yet we know that life is full of mystery and that many others have endured the same anguish.

So help us to bear our sorrow and not to question your love; for to whom can we look for comfort, but to you O Lord?

Speak your word of peace to our hearts, ease our pain and lift our darkness. Be to us a very present help in trouble, for Jesus Christ's sake.

Amen. *Frank Colquhoun*

REFLECTION

This prayer speaks to those who are suffering the agony of sudden bereavement. Its author, Frank Colquhoun, was for many years an Anglican vicar. Like all parish priests he knew that those bearing the pain of grief for a life cut short are shocked but also bewildered. That is why they often ask questions like: 'How could God let this happen to us?'

There are no easy answers to such questions. The prayer admits this, saying *our minds are baffled, our spirits weighed down with grief... It is beyond our understanding why this life should be taken.*

Inexplicable suffering and God's apparent inconsistency in allowing it to happen are among the greatest mysteries of faith. In our mortal lifetimes we shall never solve the mystery. However, Martin Luther, who perhaps more than any other Christian writer focused on the sufferings of Christ and the suffering people of Christ, emphasised that we must not limit our understanding of the power and presence of God to what we ourselves experience in times of our own suffering.

For just as those present at the crucifixion did not recognise that God was present at and sharing in that dreadful scene, let alone that he was capable of bringing something good out of it, so we do not realise that God can be present at and sharing in our dreadful scenes of suffering.

Such theological guidance is unlikely to provide immediate comfort to those who mourn. In the acute period of bereavement it is a higher priority to keep prayerful and loving lines of communication to God open and free from bitterness. This prayer so asks, adding a final appeal for Christ to bring peace, an easing of pain and to be a very present help in trouble.

Five Prayers for those that Mourn

[1]

Almighty God, Father of all mercies and giver of all comfort. Deal graciously we pray with those who mourn, that casting all their care on you they may know the consolation of your love; through Jesus Christ Our Lord.

Amen.   *Book of Common Prayer*
                                                              (1928)

[2]

Heavenly Father, God of all consolation, in your unending love and mercy for us you turn the darkness of death into the dawn of a new life.

Show compassion to your people in their sorrow. Be our refuge and our strength to lift us from the darkness of this grief to the peace and light of your presence.

Your Son, our Lord Jesus Christ, by dying for us conquered death and by rising again restored life. May we then go forward eagerly to meet him and after our life on earth, may we be recruited with our brothers and sisters where every tear will be wiped away.

We ask this through Christ our Lord.

Amen.   *Roman Missal*

REFLECTION

'Blessed are those who mourn for they shall be comforted' (Matthew 5:4), said Jesus at the beginning of the Sermon on the Mount. Throughout his earthly ministry he showed special compassion for the bereaved. He knew what it was like to mourn for he shed tears at the tomb of his friend Lazarus. So often does his comforting love flow into our lives in times of sorrow that scripture rightly describes him as 'the God of all comfort' (2 Corinthians 1:3).

Times of sorrow don't come any harder than when we have to face the death of a loved one. However strongly we believe that there is a life after death and that we shall see each other again in God's heavenly kingdom, there is still a time for weeping, mourning and anguishing over the pain of our earthly loss. This is holy ground.

When Jesus was comforting his disciples after telling them of his imminent death, he said the great words:

'Do not let your hearts be troubled. Trust in God; trust also in me. In my Father's house are many rooms; if it were not so I would have told you. I am going there to prepare a place for you. And if I go and prepare a place for you I will come back and take you to be with me that you also may be where I am.' (John 14:1–3)

In that same discourse recorded in John 14, Jesus told his disciples that he was leaving behind him the Holy Spirit. 'He will be in you. I will not leave you as orphans,' said Jesus. One of the names he gave to the Holy Spirit was 'the Comforter'.

[3]

Dear Lord Jesus, you cried when your friend Lazarus died so you understand how we are feeling today. Comfort us as we are sad and lonely without the one we loved so much. Help us to be glad that our friend is happy with you and free for ever from sadness and pain. Teach us to trust and love you so that we too may live with you for ever.

Amen.   *Anon.*

[4]

We give back to you, O God, those whom you gave to us. You did not lose them when you gave them to us and we do not lose them by their return to you.

Your Son has taught us that life is eternal and love cannot die, so death is only an horizon and an horizon is only the limit of our sight. Open our eyes to see more clearly and draw us close to you that we may know that we are nearer to our loved ones, who are with you. You have told us that you are preparing a place for us; prepare us also for that happy place, that where you are we may also be always. O Lord of life and death.

William Penn
1644–1718

[5]

O Lord God, out of the depths we cry to you. Lord, be attentive to our cry for mercy. At this time of our heartbreaking loss, let us find in your Son comfort in our sadness, certainty in our doubt, and courage to live through this hour. Make our faith strong, through Jesus Christ our Lord.

Amen.   *Roman Missal*

However broken-hearted we may be in the hour of bereavement we know from the experience of others who have suffered the loss of a loved one that our pain will gradually heal. For a time, sometimes for a long time, this seems impossible. Prayer is the healing balm we can apply to our wounds. In their different ways these five prayers offer us glimpses of God's comfort.

The prayers from the Anglican and Roman Catholic service books are traditional in their language and universal in their appeal. We do indeed need *courage to live through this hour, strength to lift us from the darkness of this grief to the peace and light of your presence and the consolation of your love*. William Penn's 17th-century prayer expresses the comforting thought that *death is only an horizon*. The modern prayer by an anonymous author reminds us that in the middle of our tears we may need to offer thanks that the deceased friend or relative is *happy with you and free for ever from sadness and pain*.

Sometimes these prayers for those who mourn help a great deal. At other times they barely register as a way of softening grief. Yet whatever the apparent result the prayer effort to offer consolation to the bereaved should be made. The last of the five prayers opens with the famous line from Psalm 130: *Out of the depths we cry to you. Lord be attentive to our cry for mercy*. St Augustine, who loved this psalm, wrote of these words: 'When we cry to our Lord from the depths he heareth our cry and the very cry itself suffereth us to move from the bottom.' What this means, in the context of bereavement, is that praying for those who mourn can start the process of God's healing and lift them from the bottom of their depths of grief.

John Donne's Vision of Heaven

Bring us, O Lord God, at our last awakening into the house and gate of heaven, to enter into that gate and dwell in that house, where there shall be no darkness nor dazzling, but one equal light; no noise nor silence, but one equal music; no fears nor hopes, but one equal possession; no ends nor beginnings, but one equal eternity: in the habitations of your majesty and glory, world without end.

Amen.

John Donne
(1572–1631)

REFLECTION

'What is heaven and who will get into it?' was one of the more intriguing essay titles set for students of theology during my years at Wycliffe Hall, Oxford.

Apart from coming up with the unoriginal conclusion that heaven is where God dwells and that its population will be full of surprises, the rest was speculation. Scripture does not help us all that much, although the book of Revelation may offer one or two heavenly glimpses. So we might as well use our celestial imaginations as so many great spiritual writers have done throughout the ages.

John Donne's vision of heaven is immensely attractive. The equality of eternity, as he portrays it, seems restful, peaceful and beautiful. *No darkness, nor dazzling ... no noise nor silence ... no fears nor hopes ...* Yet he incorporates the important concept that heaven is a house inhabited by God in all his majesty and glory.

Elsewhere in his writings John Donne made the additional point that heaven will be free of distractions from God. He once tried to write a poem about heaven only to abandon it in exasperation.

'I throw myself down in my chamber and I call in and invite God and his angels thither. But when they are here I neglect God and his angels for the noise of a fly, for the rattling of a coach, for the whining of a door,' he complained.

Such earthly grumbles, when put alongside Donne's sublime thoughts in this prayer about what he thinks we shall find at *our last awakening*, are a nice illustration of the gulf between earth and heaven. No comparison is possible. Let the last word in this book of prayers come from St Paul: 'No eye has seen, no ear has heard, no mind has conceived what God has prepared for those who love him' (1 Corinthians 2:9).

ACKNOWLEDGEMENTS

Every effort has been made to contact the copyright owners of the works reproduced in this collection. In some cases this has proven difficult. We welcome communication from any party where permission has not been cleared, and will make any necessary amendments and acknowledgements in any future edition of the book.

'The Love Song of J. Alfred Prufrock', from *Collected Poems 1909–1962* by T. S. Eliot. Reproduced by permission of Faber and Faber Ltd.

'Prayers from the Heart' and 'A Prayer to Grow in Faith', from *Prayers from the Heart* by Richard Foster. Published by Hodder & Stoughton Ltd.

'Forgive Us for Spoiling Life at Home' and 'A Prayer for Self Control', by William Barclay from *A Plain Man's Book of Prayers*.

'How Not to Pray', by John Betjeman from his *Collected Poems*. Published by John Murray, a division of Hodder Headline.

'No Excuses', by John Baillie from *A Diary of Prayer* by John Baillie. Published by Oxford University Press, UK.

'Help me to Pray', from *Letters and Papers from Prison* by Dietrich Bonhoeffer. SCM Press, 1971.

'A Prayer in Times of Sudden Bereavement', by Frank Colquhon taken from *The SPCK Book of Christian Prayer*. Used by permission of SPCK.

'The Prayer of Commitment', by Nicky Gumbel. Reproduced by permission of Holy Trinity Brompton.

Charles Colson's 'Prayer for those in Prison'. Reproduced by permission of Charles Colson.

'A Prayer for the United States Senate', by Peter Marshall, taken from *Senate Prayers of Peter Marshall*. Published by Chapman Billies, Inc. Material in the public domain.

'In Times of Pain', by Jane Grayshon. Used by permission of the author.

'Paradox of Repentance', from *A Book of Prayers*. Published by
    The Banner of Truth.
'A Prayer for our Pain to Become Our Healing', from the *Roman
    Missal*, (c) 1972, International Committee on English in the
    Liturgy, Inc. All rights reserved.
'A Prayer for Prisoners of Conscience', © Amnesty International.

Finally I would particularly like to thank Jackie Cottrell and Juliet
Sloggett who typed the manuscript, and Sacha Bonsor who helped
me with some of the historical research. My deepest gratitude
goes to the many friends and prayer partners, far too numerous
to mention by name, who have prayed these prayers with me in
recent years.